Taylor's Pocket Guide to

Old-fashioned
Roses

MAGGIE OSTER
Consulting Editor

D0033024

A Chanticleer Press Edition

Houghton Mifflin Company

Boston

Copyright © 1989 by Houghton Mifflin Company
All rights reserved.

For information about
permission to reproduce selections from this book,
write to Permissions,
Houghton Mifflin Company, 2 Park Street,
Boston, Massachusetts 02108.

Based on Taylor's Encyclopedia of Gardening, Fourth Edition,
Copyright © 1961 by Norman Taylor,
revised and edited by
Gordon P. DeWolf, Jr.

Prepared and produced by Chanticleer Press, New York
Typeset by Dix Type, Inc., Syracuse, New York
Printed and bound by
Dai Nippon, Tokyo, Japan

Library of Congress Catalog Card Number: 88-46145
ISBN: 0-395-51015-5

00   10   9   8   7   6   5   4   3   2   1

CONTENTS

GARDENING WITH
OLD-FASHIONED ROSES

ROSES are the ultimate plants of legend, romance, and beauty. They have the distinction of being among the oldest cultivated ornamental plants found in today's gardens. Throughout history, roses have figured prominently in literature, art, and medicine, as well as in horticulture. More than 2,000 years have passed since the Greek poetess Sappho christened the rose the "queen of flowers." The course of history clearly bears out this appellation, for the irresistible charm of these flowers has not diminished over the centuries.

Today roses are universally loved for the delicacy of their velvety petals, the exquisite beauty of the unfurling buds, the strength and brilliance of their colorful blooms, their heavenly fragrance, and their pure, unrivaled elegance. Despite their delicate appearance, roses are long-lived, strong, rugged plants. The roses in this book are well suited to beginning gardeners, who will find that a little time and effort can be most beautifully rewarded.

Classification of Roses

A rose is assigned to a particular class on the basis of its ancestry and, in certain cases, on how long it has been in cultivation. The old-fashioned roses, often called heritage roses, comprise four classes: species roses, climbing roses, shrub roses, and old garden roses. From the point of view of the beginning gardener, the class to which a rose belongs does not make an enormous difference; but there are distinctions in hardiness, habit, and size that may influence your decision when purchasing rose bushes. In this book, the individual plant descriptions are arranged according to class, and organized by flower color and shape within each class.

Species Roses

Natural wild roses—commonly called species roses—grow throughout the Northern Hemisphere, from North America to Europe, China, and Japan. They are known to thrive in a very wide range of habitats and climates, flourishing from the far North down to the northern reaches of Africa. Each wild rose has a two-part scientific, or Latin, name. The first part, the generic name, tells us that the plants belong to a group of related plants all in the genus *Rosa*. The second part is the species name; *Rosa rugosa* and *Rosa multiflora* are species. (In contrast, most of the other roses in this book are varieties or hybrids, and they bear names, such as Harison's Yellow, Madame Hardy, or Dublin Bay, given them by breeders.)

Species roses are for the most part once-blooming, and most of them flower early in the season, in May or June. They produce an enormous crop of blossoms each year. In most instances, the flowers are followed by brightly colored fruits, known as seed hips, that prolong the beauty of the plants and provide food for birds. Rose hips also make attractive subjects for flower and foliage arrangements.

Species roses require little care in the garden. Many of these vigorous roses are also extremely hardy, although it is well to remember that some are more naturally cold-tolerant than others. If you do decide to plant species roses in your garden, make certain that you have allowed enough room for these vigorous plants. Many of them are extremely bushy and will grow up to eight or nine feet tall and just as wide.

As garden subjects, species roses are delightful and varied. Some—especially the larger varieties—are ideally suited for hedges, while others are very sprawling in their growth and make a good ground cover. Individual bushes or a row of species roses will make a very fine backdrop for many other plants, including other types of roses.

Climbers

Left to grow on their own, climbing roses do not actually climb at all—they lack the tendrils that true climbing plants, such as vines, use to attach themselves to structures. The long, supple or sturdy canes must be tied to a support, such as a trellis or a wall. There climbers serve a variety of purposes, covering ugly structures or forming beautiful arbors. There are seven different groups of climbing roses, but only five are widely grown. Distinguishing among the groups is by no means essential, but may be of interest.

The **climbing hybrid teas** are mostly sports, or chance mutations, of the bush varieties of hybrid tea roses, although there are a few climbing hybrid teas for which there is no bush form. Both types resemble other hybrid tea roses in every way, being medium-sized, upright, rather stiffly caned plants.

The winter-hardy **kordesii climbers** are medium-sized roses with intensely colored, well-shaped blooms and dark, holly-like foliage. They make wonderful pillar roses (that is, grown up onto a post) and are perfect for planting along a fence.

The **large-flowered climbers** are a catch-all group. These roses have medium-sized to large blooms, usually in small clusters. Some large-flowered climbers are repeat bloomers, but others are not.

Derived from the Memorial Rose, *Rosa wichuraiana*, the **hybrid wichuraiana climbers** are large, strong climbers, with canes reaching as long as 20 feet or more. Their foliage is shining, dark green, and disease proof. The sweetly scented blooms are large and well shaped, in shades of white or pink. Wichuraiana climbers are once-blooming; some varieties have a pleasing hip display later in the fall.

Rambler roses are the last of the climbers to come into bloom. They are once-blooming, but they extend the rose season with very bright colors of pink, red, and purple. Ramblers have long, pliable canes that can easily be trained to a trellis or fence. They are not the best choices for walls, being in the main very susceptible to mildew; good air circulation is a must. Ramblers bear many tiny flowers in huge clusters. These usually come on second-year canes, so it is a good idea to prune away the oldest canes each year. Pruning is easiest in late winter or early spring, when the plants are just coming out of dormancy and there is no foliage to hide the canes.

Shrub Roses

Like many terms used in horticulture, the word "shrub" is open to a number of different interpretations. For the purposes of this book, the shrub roses include several subclasses.

Descended from *Rosa eglanteria,* the **hybrid eglantines** were developed by Lord Penzance in the late 1800s. They make upright, treelike shrubs, with flowers a little larger than those produced by the species. Unfortunately, the foliage is not fragrant and plants tend to get black spot. They do offer a good range of colors and garden uses.

The **hybrid musk** roses are a 20th-century development, descendants of *Rosa multiflora.* Resembling the blowsy, overgrown floribundas, they can be used as big, freestanding bushes or hedges, or trained as low climbers. The blooms are mostly delicate shades that quickly fade to white, although there are a few in deeper tones. Most varieties are fragrant. Hybrid musks have exceptionally good repeat bloom in full sun. A few varieties have attractive fall hips.

The **hybrid rugosas,** another 20th-century group, are a varied lot. Some have the deeply etched foliage typical of the wild roses, while others do not. Some produce good repeat blooms while others have neither repeat blooms nor good hip displays. Some are also borderline winter hardy.

There are two categories of **hybrid spinosissimas,** descendants of *Rosa spinosissima.* The first includes ancient varieties and is grouped with the old garden roses. The second includes the modern shrub hybrid spinosissimas, particularly the "Frühlings series" developed by Wilhelm Kordes. These latter ones are upright, arching bushes, rather open and gaunt in habit, with very early blooms. The very large, sweetly fragrant flowers are mostly single, but some varieties are fully double. Plants grow seven to nine feet tall.

The **polyantha** roses (from the Greek for "many-flowered") started out as everblooming dwarf forms of once-blooming climbing and rambling roses. Most are very hardy, neat little shrubs in many colors. They make a bright accent in the garden and are very dependable.

Finally, there is a catch-all category, called simply **shrub** roses. These descendants of older shrub roses are modern varieties—having come into cultivation after the mid-19th century—that cannot be classified with any of the other shrub-rose groups.

Old Garden Roses

Forming a very large class, the old garden roses have been in cultivation for centuries. Although their popularity had begun to wane in the 19th century, these old fashioned-looking flowers are once more being widely grown. The old garden roses are really a "super-class." Included under that heading are the following classes, distinguished chiefly by their parentage: alba, Bourbon, centifolia, China, damask, gallica, hybrid perpetual, hybrid spinosissima (in part), moss, Noisette, Portland, and tea.

Producing very fragrant white or pale pink blooms, the **alba** roses are tall and upright. The foliage is soft and downy, and the canes are rather thorny. They bloom once a year.

A natural hybrid, *Rosa borboniana* was discovered on the Isle of Bourbon (now Réunion Island), where farmers hedged their fields with China and damask roses—its parents. The **Bourbon** roses are decendants of this hybrid. Taller and more vigorous than either parent, and with a much larger bloom, the moderately hardy Bourbons produce shapely blossoms throughout the summer.

The **centifolia** roses are varieties and hybrids of *Rosa centifolia*, which is believed to have been developed in Holland during the 17th and 18th centuries, and found also in the Provence region of France. Centifolia roses bloom once, bearing double and very full-petaled flowers with an intense perfume. The large outer petals enclose many tightly packed inner petals; there is often a "button" center, and the petals often arrange themselves into four radial segments (they are said to be "quartered"). The very thorny, long canes spring up in all directions, bearing sparse foliage.

European explorers of the late 1700s and early 1800s collected some very important China roses and tea-scented China roses. Unlike European roses, these newly discovered roses were capable of dependable repeat flowering.

The **China** roses bear loosely cup-shaped blooms that tend to darken in the sun instead of fading; the flowers shatter cleanly when fully expanded and aged. Chinas have very smooth stems and leaves. They are not very winter hardy, but being fairly small plants may be grown in pots indoors in the winter.

The **tea** roses have loosely cupped blooms in delicate shades and blends of white, pink, and pale yellow. They are very smooth, with glossy leaves and few real thorns. The teas are the roses that, crossed with the hybrid perpetuals, gave us our hybrid tea roses.

Hybrids of *Rosa damascena,* the **damask** roses are among the most ancient of garden roses. Grown throughout the Roman Empire, they would have died out in medieval times had it not been for the hundreds of monasteries across Europe, where roses and many other flowers were grown for medicinal purposes and thus preserved.

Damasks require careful cultivation. They are mostly very thorny shrubs, with blooms in clusters of three or five; some varieties are repeat bloomers. The cup-shaped, intensely fragrant flowers sometimes cannot open fully because of the tight petal clusters.

The **gallica** roses are descended from *Rosa gallica* and were also known to the Romans. Varieties appear in deep shades of pink, sometimes striped or mottled with lighter pink, sometimes shading into lavender and violet; some of the deepest of purples are also found among the gallicas. All these rich shades are enhanced by showy yellow stamens. The tidy, neat, upright gallicas are fragrant—remarkably more so when the petals are dried. Gallicas are once-blooming and produce attractive hips later in the season.

The **hybrid perpetuals,** forerunners of our modern hybrid teas, are of mixed ancestry, descended mainly from teas, Bourbons, and Portlands. The heyday of their popularity was from 1840 to 1880, but these roses were grown before that time and long afterward. There is great variation in flower form, from very full-petaled, "old-garden" blooms to high-centered flowers resembling the hybrid teas.

The **hybrid spinosissimas,** also known as Scotch, burnet, and pimpinellifolia roses, are varieties of *Rosa spinosissima.* Most roses of this lineage are shrub roses, but some of the older varieties are ancient and thus classed as old garden roses. The Scotch roses were ferny, low-growing shrubs, with surprisingly well-formed blooms. The most notable variety, and the only one that currently produces a good repeat bloom, is Stanwell Perpetual, growing in low mounds of fernlike foliage with fragrant flowers.

The **moss** roses are a single group derived from two sources: those that are sports, or mutations, of the centifolias, and those that sported from the damask perpetuals. The former have heavy green moss on the bud and stems, while the latter have rather sparse, brownish moss, and bloom a second time in the fall. Moss roses were very popular during Victorian times. The buds have a pine scent that further enhances the pleasure of the intensely fragrant, fully double blooms.

Named for a famous rose breeder, the **Noisettes** originated from a chance cross between China and musk roses in the early 1800s. They flourish in warm climates but are not winter hardy, so they have never become popular except in those areas best suited to them.

The **Portland** roses, sometimes called damask perpetuals, are descended from the autumn damask, gallica, and China roses; they were an early 19th-century attempt at developing repeat-blooming roses. Today there are few varieties left, but those that survive are very good repeat bloomers with neat, round growth, and smooth stems and foliage. The blooms are very fragrant; when fully expanded, the outer petals curl in on themselves, creating fluffy balls.

Getting Started

For many centuries and in many diverse cultures, roses have been grown in small beds in enclosed gardens. This formal type of rose garden, composed of symmetrical beds, perhaps edged with white- or dark-leaved plants, set against a hedge of dark evergreens, and with a fountain, statue, gazebo, or other focal point, is what many people associate with roses.

Yet roses can be used in many other ways in the landscape. If you like natural abandon, cover your house and outbuildings with old-fashioned climbers, and mix your roses with other flowers, cottage-garden style. Large shrub roses, and some of the older varieties, will need a good deal of space and are appropriately grouped in wide borders. Climbers can also be trained on posts as "pillar" roses, grown laterally along a fence, or literally up a tree. Roses can be beautifully arrayed in rows beside a path, either alone or with an edging of another plant. You can even create meandering paths through large rose bushes, or arrange various roses in free-form, curving beds.

Purchasing Rose Bushes

The first important consideration in growing beautiful roses, and one that is often overlooked by the beginner, is to start out with good plants. To be sure of obtaining good, healthy plants, it is a smart idea to purchase your roses either from a reputable mail-order company or from a local nursery or garden store.

Don't assume that high-priced roses are necessarily the best. The price of patented, newer hybrids includes a royalty; older varieties or cultivars, which have stood the test of time, may do just as well and are often less expensive.

The American Rose Society publishes a booklet called the "Handbook for Selecting Roses," which rates all roses on a scale from 1 to 10, based on members' comments. This too is a good guide in selecting varieties; any variety rated over 7.5 would be a good choice. Members also receive a monthly magazine and an annual yearbook. The Society has many other programs of benefit to rose growers; contact them at P.O. Box 30,000, Shreveport, LA 71130 for further information.

Roses are graded (1, 1½, or 2) in accordance with established standards laid down in 1923 and revised periodically since then. The highest grade is Grade 1, but whichever you purchase, be sure that the plant you buy has a robust, well-developed root system. The canes should not be shriveled or blackened or show any other sign of damage; the bark should be green and the pith white or nearly white. Look for healthy growth or growth buds. If you purchase Grade 1½ roses, you should pay less for these than you would for Grade 1 plants.

Soil Analysis

After you have determined where to plant your bushes, take a sample of your soil and have it analyzed at a local soil-testing laboratory or by a state agricultural college. The testing facility will provide instructions for taking a sample.

The soil test report will suggest the amounts of nitrogen, phosphorus, and potassium (also called potash) that will need to be added to your soil. The report will also give your soil's pH—the acidity or alkalinity of the soil. A pH of 7 is neutral; a higher pH indicates alkaline soil, and a lower one acid soil. Roses prefer a slightly acid soil with a pH of 6.5 to 6.8, but will grow in soil from pH 6 to 7.5. To raise the pH level, you add agricultural lime or dolomitic limestone; to decrease it, you add sulfur. Your County Extension Service or local garden center can advise you on how much to add.

Location

Roses need at least six hours of sunlight each day. If there is a choice of morning or afternoon sun, choose the morning. In addition, roses must have good air circulation but not harsh wind. Also, do not plant too close to existing trees and shrubs, which will compete for water and nutrients. Choose a site with deep, fertile, well-drained soil.

Spacing Your Roses

The distance between each bush depends on climate and the plant itself. Crowding makes it easy for insects and fungus disease to thrive and spread. The roses in this book should be planted four to ten feet apart, depending on the growth habit of the plants involved. Roses are spaced farther apart in southern states than in northern areas.

Preparing the Bed

The best time to prepare a new rose bed is in the fall, so that the materials added to the soil can begin their work and be settled before spring planting. If there is grass sod on the surface, remove a two-inch layer and use it where needed in your yard. Now loosen the soil with a spade to a depth of 18–20 inches. Next, work some compost, peat moss, or well-rotted cow manure into the soil. Use about 12 cubic feet of peat moss per 100 square feet of soil. If the soil has less than the required amount of phosphorus, then add 15 pounds of bone meal or three or four pounds of 20-percent superphosphate per 100 square feet.

These are general recommendations, and it would be best to check with a consulting rosarian from your local rose society, the County Extension Agent, or a local garden center for specific advice for your area.

Planting Bare-Root Roses

Bare-root roses may be bought locally or by mail-order, and are planted in early spring. If you cannot plant them immediately, keep them wrapped and stored in a cool, dark place. At planting time, place your rose bushes in a tub of warm water that covers the canes as well as the roots, and let them soak for a couple of hours. When you are ready to plant, remove the bushes from the water, examine the roots and canes, and remove any damaged or dead ones with your pruning shears.

For each bush, dig a hole at least 18 inches wide and deep. Form a mound of soil in the center of the hole. Place the plant on this mound, spreading the roots out as evenly as possible. The crown, or bud union—the knot of wood between the canes and the roots—should be one or two inches below the soil level in the North, where temperatures fall below zero during the winter, and one or two inches above the soil level in southern climates. Orient the plant so that the sides of the bud union from which most of the canes grow will face north. This causes new canes to form on the south side, producing a more rounded bush.

Fill in the hole with soil until it is about three-fourths full, tamping or firming the soil with your hands. Add water to the hole, filling it to the top. Let it soak into the soil. Fill the rest of the hole with soil and water again.

If you live in the North, mound soil over the newly planted bush to a height of 10–12 inches (less if the canes are short). Thoroughly dampen this mound. In several weeks or less, leaves and stems will sprout. At that time, gradually over a week, remove the mound by gently washing with a hose or watering can.

Planting Potted Roses

Dig a hole as described previously. Fill in with enough soil so the bud union will be at the proper depth. Soak the soil in the pot, then gently remove the plant from the pot, grasping it firmly at the soil level. Set into the hole and fill in around the root ball with soil. Tamp lightly and water well.

Fertilizers and Feeding

Beginners will find that there are many materials and methods of fertilizing. What constitutes the best method is a matter of opinion, so just make sure you do fertilize your roses during the growing season. Choosing a fertilizer specially formulated for roses is the simplest solution. When you buy fertilizer, three numbers are printed on the bag or container, such as 10–10–10, 18–6–12, or 5–10–10. These represent the percentage (by weight) of the nitrogen, phosphorus, and potassium included in the mixture.

For newly planted rose bushes, add fertilizer only after the first blooming cycle and thereafter only once a month. Stop feeding roses six weeks before the last bloom cycle, or about eight weeks before the first frost. Scatter the fertilizer evenly around the bush, at least six inches from the base. Scratch it lightly into the soil, and then water it in. If your soil is dry, water the soil the day before you feed. On two-year-old or established rose bushes, feeding should start in the spring about four to six weeks before the first cycle of blooms, with continued feeding as discussed above.

Mulching

Some gardeners like mulch, while others do not, but mulching does keep weeds in check, conserves water, and keeps the soil cool. In addition, an organic mulch will slowly contribute to the humus in the soil. The best time to apply mulch is after the soil has warmed but before bushes start growing, when the soil is moist. Apply a four-inch layer of an organic material, such as shredded bark, cocoa bean hulls, ground corncobs, or half-rotted compost.

Pruning

To have strong, healthy rose bushes, it is essential to learn how to prune them. Buy a good pair of scissors-type pruning shears, or secateurs; cheap shears and anvil-type shears will damage your bushes. In general, the majority of old-fashioned roses need only to have dead or diseased wood removed or general shaping. The albas, centifolias, damasks, and gallicas benefit from a summer pruning after flowering, removing dead, diseased, weak, crisscrossing, or overcrowded canes.

On repeat-blooming roses, after a bush has bloomed, the next step is to remove the spent blooms. This process is called "dead-heading." Cut the bloom at the stem, about one-quarter inch above the first pair of five-leaflet leaves that faces toward the outside of the bush. Continue this practice throughout the growing season to encourage more blooms.

Late winter and early spring pruning is essential for established plants of Portlands, hybrid musks, Bourbons, hybrid perpetuals, Chinas, and teas. Remove dead, diseased, damaged, or broken canes as well as canes that cross through the center of the bush and rub against another cane. Also remove any weak or very thin canes. Finally, cut the tallest canes back by a third, and shorter growth by two-thirds.

As you prune, be sure to examine the color of the canes' center, or pith, which is white when healthy. If your first pruning does not reach healthy pith, continue cutting. Always cut back to an outward-facing bud eye; the cutting angle should be 45 degrees.

It is advisable to seal all cut canes against insects, especially borers. Use fingernail polish, white household glue, carbolated Vaseline, or a tree-wound compound.

Rugosas should only be lightly pruned to maintain their shape. But if growth gets out of hand, they will tolerate severe pruning.

After pruning, clean up all debris and old leaves to keep diseases from spreading. It is a good idea to spray the bushes and ground with a fungicide at this time, to kill any fungus spores that may be present.

Pruning Climbers

In terms of pruning, climbers are of two types. The ramblers can have the ends of the long canes snipped to produce more lateral stems and blooms next year. Some gardeners also prefer to cut ramblers back to the ground as soon as the bush has finished flowering. Doing this allows new canes to grow during the summer from which blooms are produced during the next year. Nearly all the ramblers produce flowers only on second-year wood.

With both once- and repeat-blooming large-flowered climbers, you need only prune old, nonproductive canes and winter dieback. The repeat bloomers should have the short flowering stems cut back to the first set of five-leaflet leaves as soon as the flowers are spent. Be sure to remove faded flowers.

Winterizing

In the fall, three to five weeks before the first hard frost in your area, refrain from cutting the spent blooms. Even though roses in the Deep South may not go dormant, leaving the spent blooms on in November gives the plants a rest. In January, you can begin pruning for the coming year.

You should also withhold any nitrogen-containing fertilizer six to ten weeks before the last blooming cycle.

The most common way to protect roses is to take soil from a location other than the rose bed and make a mound around the base of the plant to a height of 10–12 inches. Where temperatures remain below freezing for some time and the weather becomes stabilized, additional protection is needed. You can use leaves, wood chips, pine needles, bark, sawdust, and ground corncobs. Do not apply until weather is consistently cold. Tie the canes to keep them from breaking in strong winds. Some gardeners use rose cones made of plastic foam, or collars that contain mulch.

In the North, climbing roses need extra protection. Mounding soil on the base will help, and wrapping the canes in burlap will protect them from drying out. You may also dig a trench next to the bush and bend the canes into the trench, covering them with soil or other material.

Old-Fashioned Elegance

Now you have at your fingertips all the facts you will need to bring the true elegance of old-fashioned roses into your garden. Whether you opt for the romantic, full blooms of the old garden roses or the sturdy, simple brilliance of the species roses, you will be sure to find within the pages of this book just the right flowers. So, turn to the individual descriptions and prepare to delight yourself and your friends with the luscious beauty of old-fashioned roses.

Old-fashioned Roses

The Rugosa Rose, its sports, and its natural and man-made hybrids are among the most important roses for the garden. Among the most adaptable and disease free of all roses, they bloom throughout the season. Several have petals with frilled edges.

Garden Profile

The single to double flowers are a medium mauve-pink and intensely fragrant. Buds open to reveal wide, crinkly, cupped petals and golden stamens. Plants have upright, vigorous growth, reaching at least 3–5 feet tall; in the right conditions, they will grow much taller. The canes are very thorny. The wrinkly, deeply etched leaves are dark green, leathery, and glossy. In the fall, they turn bronze, then bright yellow. The large, orange-red hips, like small cherry tomatoes, are edible. They persist well into winter. This rose prefers sandy soils, but it is adaptable, if less vigorous, in almost any site. Disease free and winter hardy.

Like *R. rugosa alba,* this wild rose is a chance mutation, or sport, of *Rosa rugosa.* The parent species was brought to North America in the middle of the 19th century; it has since become widely naturalized. *Rosa rugosa rubra* has brilliant blooms all season long and makes a good hedge. The hips, which are set in fall, are edible, and they can be made into jams, jellies, syrups, and other confections.

GARDEN PROFILE

The single flowers are deep mauve pink, with 5–12 petals. Intensely fragrant, they bloom all summer. Bright red hips form later in the season. The plants grow upright; spreading and dense, they reach 3–5 feet in height. The leaves are glossy and leathery; dark green, they are etched with deep lines. The canes are very thorny. Disease free and winter hardy.

Rosa eglanteria (Species)

This rose is the Sweetbriar, or Eglantine, of Shakespeare and other writers. Over the years there have been both natural and man-made hybrids, double and single, and in shades of white, red, deep pink, and pink and yellow bicolor. The most notable were the Penzance hybrids, developed in England by Lord Penzance during the 1890s. A few are still available from old-rose specialist nurseries.

GARDEN PROFILE

Light to medium pink flowers, 1–1½ inches wide, bloom in clusters, opening flat to reveal showy yellow stamens. Plants bloom once, early in the season, and have a light, sweet, true-rose fragrance. Clusters of hips ripen to a bright red in fall and remain well into winter. The leaves are small, abundant, medium green, and glossy, with a fragrance of apples. The upright, vigorous plants grow 8–10 feet tall. Plants are winter hardy and disease resistant, but some hybrids may be susceptible to black spot and mildew.

Rosa rubrifolia (Species)

The unusual metallic, gray-green leaves, overlain with the dusky color of plums, have made this rose popular for borders and flower arrangements. It was one of the roses grown by Empress Josephine at Malmaison. This rose works well in perennial or shrub borders where red, brown, pink, and purple predominate; it is also an excellent hedge rose.

GARDEN PROFILE

The single pink flowers, borne in small clusters, have a white center with yellow stamens. Only ½ inch across, the fragrant blooms appear early in the season with no repeat. Small, shiny, dark red hips appear in fall. Plants grow 4–8 feet tall; the size depends greatly on the strain. Growth is upright, open, and gracefully arching. The smooth, almost thornless canes are red-brown.

Rosa rugosa alba (Species)

A white sport, or chance mutation, of *Rosa rugosa,* this bloomer is very similar to its relative in everything but color. Sometimes called the Salt Spray Rose, it grows wild on the beaches and other seaside areas of North America, where it helps to stabilize dunes. In the garden, its intense fragrance and lustrous flowers are always a welcome addition.

Garden Profile

Flowers are white, single, with 5–12 petals; they grow to 2½–3½ inches across and have a strong clove fragrance. Bloom is continuous throughout most of the season; bright orange-red hips are set after the flowering is finished. The upright, vigorous, spreading plants form a dense bush. The leaves are dark green and leathery; the canes are very thorny. This wild rose is disease free and winter hardy.

Although this species is most notable for its importance in the hybridization of climbing roses, *Rosa wichuraiana* can stand on its own merits in the garden as a ground cover or climbing rose. Allowed to grow prostrate, *R. wichuraiana* forms a dense mat by sending out roots wherever it touches the ground. It is used as a ground cover in cemeteries and is sometimes called the Memorial Rose.

GARDEN PROFILE

Plants bloom once a year late in the season, most often July or August, bearing clusters of white, fragrant flowers 1½–2 inches wide. Small red, oval hips appear later in the season. Growing 10–20 feet long, the dark brown, flexible canes can also be trained upright on supports. This rose is particularly attractive growing up into a tree, with the branches cascading down. The medium-sized foliage is dark green and glossy. In milder climates, it is evergreen. This rose is disease free and hardy in all but very severe climates.

Found growing wild throughout much of eastern North America, *Rosa multiflora* is sometimes sold as a "living fence" by nurseries, so dense and compact is its growth. It grows so aggressively that in some places it is considered a weed. With proper control, however, it can be a nice addition to the garden. It is in the ancestry of many polyanthas and floribundas.

GARDEN PROFILE

Flowers are white, single, with 5 petals; just ½ inch wide, they bloom in large, airy clusters from early in the season to midseason. They have a honey fragrance. Tiny round red hips follow later. Plants grow 7–12 feet tall, with upright, arching canes. The leaves are light to medium green, long, narrow, and glossy. *Rosa multiflora* is disease free and winter hardy in all but the most severe climates.

Rosa hugonis (Species)

Fr. Hugh Scanlon, 1899

Father Hugo's Rose, or the Golden Rose of China, was discovered by Father Hugh Scanlon, a French missionary, at the end of the 19th century. He sent seeds to Kew Gardens in England, where the rose was raised and later distributed to other gardens and nurseries.

GARDEN PROFILE

Blooming in early spring on thin, arching brown branches, the single yellow flowers are 1½–2 inches across and cup shaped, with very showy golden stamens. Plants are tall and graceful, to 6 feet high and as wide. Flowers bloom once, early in the season, and are followed by small maroon to black hips in late summer. The leaves are small and light to medium green, with a fernlike appearance and touch; they turn an orange-bronze in fall. Poorly drained or highly fertile soils will be fatal. Prune back to live wood in the spring and remove dead or nonflowering canes as the need arises. Disease free and winter hardy except in extreme climates.

New Dawn (Climber)

Dreer, 1930

Called "the ideal, smaller rambling rose" by British rose specialist Peter Beales, New Dawn has a lovely romantic quality. A perpetual-flowering sport of Dr. W. van Fleet, it had the distinction of receiving, in 1930, the first plant patent issued in the United States. Its breeding heritage includes *R. wichuraiana* as well as tea and hybrid tea roses, and thus it is closely aligned to modern climbing hybrid teas.

GARDEN PROFILE

The clusters of delightfully fragrant, round buds open to semidouble flowers of 18–24 petals. Each blush or silvery pink flower is 3½–4 inches across. When fully open, the cupped blossoms show bright yellow stamens. Plants are upright, vigorous, and bushy, growing 12–15 feet tall. The canes are moderately thorny and the leaves are a medium, glossy green. New Dawn takes several years before it will start to climb. Given time, it makes an outstanding addition to the garden. Disease free and winter hardy.

Blossomtime (Climber)

Blossomtime is descended from another very beautiful pink climber, New Dawn. A good pillar or trellis rose, it can also be left to grow as a loose, open shrub rather than trained upright.

GARDEN PROFILE

Blossomtime bears clusters of 3–8 high-centered, classically formed flowers of clear pink with a deeper pink reverse. These very fragrant double blooms have 35–40 petals. Flowering is best in midseason, but there is some repeat bloom. The upright and vigorous plants grow 7–9 feet tall. Canes are thorny with medium green, semiglossy leaves. Disease resistant and winter hardy.

Handel (Climber)

Rose hybridizer Sam McGredy is known for producing unusually colored roses, and Handel is part of that tradition. It is an excellent choice for covering a fence, wall, or trellis.

GARDEN PROFILE

Flowers are cream to white, edged in bright pink to red; double, with 22 petals. The red edging becomes more pronounced with age and in hot weather. Starting as high-centered buds, the flowers open to a cupped form. There is a slight fragrance. The most abundant bloom is in June, but Handel produces flowers until frost, and the fall flowering is particularly lovely. The plants are very vigorous and upright; the moderately thorny, dark canes grow 12 to 15 feet tall. The glossy, medium green to dark green foliage has a purple cast. Winter hardy and disease resistant.

American Pillar (Climber)

Van Fleet, 1902

Amerian Pillar is classified with the wichuraiana climbers, a group of large, strong climbing roses; *Rosa setigera* is also in the parentage of this deep pink bloomer. Climbing roses can often serve a double purpose in the garden: they not only add beauty, but they can also be used to mask ugly outbuildings, fences, and even dead trees.

GARDEN PROFILE

The flowers of this rose are deep pink with a white eye; they are single, with 5 petals, and grow 2–3 inches across. Blooms occur in immense clusters toward the end of the season, with no repeat. Red hips appear in fall. The plants grow upright and vigorous, reaching 15–20 feet. The canes are moderately thorny, and the leaves are medium green, leathery, and glossy. American Pillar is disease resistant, but may have a problem with mildew in the South. It is winter hardy.

Lawrence Johnston

This lovely, exuberant, old-fashioned-looking rose was almost lost to us, because its creator, Joseph Pernet-Ducher, didn't deem it particularly noteworthy. Fortunately it caught the eye of an Englishman, Lawrence Johnston, who took it home to Gloucestershire and shared cuttings with his friends. It won the Royal Horticultural Society's Award of Merit in 1948. Also called Hidcote Yellow.

GARDEN PROFILE

The warm yellow flowers are 3–3½ inches across; semidouble, with 18–24 petals. Cupped blooms occur in great numbers in early summer and continue sparsely throughout the season. The plants are vigorous, growing to 20 feet, and require adequate space. The canes are thorny; the glossy leaves are medium green. Plants are winter hardy and, in most areas, disease resistant, although highly prone to black spot in the South.

City of York (Climber)

Tantau, 1945

City of York is the result of a cross between a hybrid tea rose, Prof. Gnau, and the well-known pink rambler, Dorothy Perkins. In 1950, it won the American Rose Society National Gold Medal Certificate. Because of its height, City of York can be very useful on arches and other structures.

GARDEN PROFILE
Blooming for a very long time during the middle of the growing season, the buff-yellow buds of City of York open to a creamy white with a hint of yellow in the center. Semi-double, with 15 petals, these flowers at first have their centers closed and rounded. Upon fully opening flat, the bright golden stamens at the center are revealed. The flowers are very fragrant, a trait that cannot be taken for granted among climbers. The pliable, very vigorous, moderately thorny canes can grow to 20 feet tall. Leaves are a glossy, light to medium green. Plants are disease free and winter hardy.

Joseph's Coat (Climber)

Armstrong & Swim, 1964

This rose is aptly named: when it blooms, it is clothed in a kaleidoscope of colors. Although listed as a climber, it is best used as a short pillar rose or a loose, open, freestanding shrub. Joseph's Coat won the 1964 Bagatelle Gold Medal.

Garden Profile

Shapely, golden-yellow buds open to double, 24- to 30-petaled, cupped flowers of yellow, changing to orange and red. Occurring in clusters, the loosely formed, 3- to 4-inch flowers have a slight scent. The best bloom is in midseason, with a fair repeat bloom following. Plants are upright and vigorous. The thorny canes reach 8–10 feet tall. Leaves are a dark, glossy green. Disease resistant, Joseph's Coat is not dependably winter hardy.

May Queen (Climber)

Manda, 1898

A comparatively old hybrid, this wichuraiana climber is not as vigorous as many other members of its group. Its somewhat more contained growth suits it to a variety of situations: train it up on a trellis or wall, perhaps as a backdrop to lower-growing shrub roses.

GARDEN PROFILE

The flowers are medium pink and double, with 45–55 petals, and 3–3½ inches wide. They have a fragrance of green apples. The blooms open fully to a slighty cupped form. The plants are upright and grow vigorously to 15 feet tall. The moderately thorny canes have glossy leaves. May Queen is disease free and winter hardy.

Dublin Bay (Climber)

McGredy, 1975

Bred by an Irishman, Dublin Bay has Altissimo, another excellent red climbing rose, as one parent. Dublin Bay makes a good climbing or pillar rose and can also be grown as a large, loose, open shrub.

GARDEN PROFILE

A deep, rich red, the fragrant flowers of Dublin Bay are at their most profuse during June and July. Flowers open to 4½ inches; they are double, with 25 petals. They have good repeat bloom throughout the summer. Plants have vigorous, upright growth, reaching 8–14 feet tall. The canes are moderately thorny and the large, glossy, leathery leaves are medium to dark green. Plants are disease resistant and winter hardy.

America (Climber)

A fragrant white climber, America claimed the American Rose Society National Gold Medal Certificate in 1950. It belongs to a group known as large-flowered climbers, a catch-all group of roses with medium-sized to large blooms that are usually borne in clusters. America makes a good backdrop for low-growing shrub roses.

GARDEN PROFILE

The white, semidouble flowers, with 15 petals, are 3–3½ inches wide and very fragrant. The bloom opens to a saucer shape, revealing bright yellow stamens at the center. There is a long midseason bloom, but no repeat. The plants, which are very vigorous, grow to 20 feet tall. The canes are moderately thorny; they are clothed in glossy, light green to medium green leaves. America is disease free and winter hardy.

The Fairy (Shrub)

Bentall, 1932

No aspect of life is without dissension, least of all the world of roses. The Fairy, a dainty rose of sturdy constitution, stands serenely at the center of controversy about its parentage. In addition, it is sometimes encountered as a ground-hugging trailer, and in other instances as an upright hedge. Whether the rose is variable, or the labeling imprecise, has not been determined. The origin is of minor importance to most gardeners, but the growth habit is of more concern. When possible, check with your source to determine how your Fairy will grow.

GARDEN PROFILE

This low-growing rose is covered with small flowers from summer until frost. The clusters of cupped, double, medium pink blooms have little or no scent. Each flower is 1–1½ inches wide, with 24–30 petals. The bushy, spreading plants grow 1½–2 feet tall. Moderately thorny canes bear tiny, abundant, glossy leaves, light to medium green. The Fairy is winter hardy and generally disease resistant except for occasional outbreaks of black spot or mildew. Prune after flowering to help it rebloom.

China Doll (Shrub)

China Doll belongs to a group of roses called the polyanthas—low-growing, very bushy plants that bear a great number of small flowers. China Doll is a good choice for a low edging, perhaps around other roses or along a path or driveway.

GARDEN PROFILE

The cupped blossoms are 1–2 inches wide, light to medium pink with a yellow base, and double, with 20–26 petals. The blooms first appear late in the season but continue until frost. They are lightly fragrant. Plants grow 1½ feet tall, with bushy, spreading, compact growth. The leaves are medium green and leathery. The plants are disease resistant and winter hardy.

Frühlingsgold (Shrub)

Kordes, 1937

Frühlingsgold and Frühlingsmorgen, 2 hybrid spinosissima shrub roses developed by Kordes, are descended from *Rosa spinosissima,* the Scotch Rose. These modern spinosissimas form arching hoops and make a tremendous display in early spring. Frühlingsmorgen is very similar to the variety pictured here, but has pink blooms with yellow at the base.

GARDEN PROFILE

Frühlingsgold has light yellow, single flowers with 5 petals; the fragrant blooms open to a saucer shape, 3–3½ inches wide, with showy yellow stamens. The plants are upright, arching, and vigorous, with moderately thorny canes and soft, dull, light green leaves. They are disease free and winter hardy.

Golden Wings (Shrub)

Shepherd, 1956

Almost the earliest rose to bloom, Golden Wings remains in flower longer than any other rose. A favorite of bees, it is also popular with people, and is considered the best landscape rose. This rose won the American Rose Society National Gold Medal Certificate in 1958.

GARDEN PROFILE

The large flowers, 4–5 inches across, are single, with 5 petals. They are pale yellow when they first open and gradually turn golden. The stamens may be golden-brown to orange-red. The lightly fragrant flowers are borne both in clusters and singly. The upright, vigorous, well-branched plants grow 4½–5½ feet tall. Canes are moderately thorny. The leaves are a light, dull green. Golden Wings is disease resistant and winter hardy except in very severe winter climates.

Nevada (Shrub)

Dot, 1927

Nevada was one of the first hybrids of Spanish rose breeder Pedro Dot, who went on to introduce over 120 varieties. It was long thought a moyesii hybrid, but many authorities now question this attribution. Regardless of its origins, it makes a superb specimen plant in the landscape. Noted authority Graham Stuart Thomas has called it "one of the most spectacular shrubs when in bloom."

GARDEN PROFILE

The reddish buds open to single, 5-petaled flowers, 3½–4 inches wide. Saucer shaped with yellow stamens, the creamy white blooms may be tinged with pink during hot weather or in the fall. They have little or no fragrance, but excellent repeat bloom. Plants grow vigorously to 6–8 feet tall and as wide, with arching red-brown branches. Canes have few thorns. The leaves are small, semiglossy, and a soft, gray-green. Nevada is winter hardy and disease resistant.

Cornelia (Shrub)

Pemberton, 1925

Although research indicates that the rose originally introduced in 1925 under this name is not the same as the rose sold today, the "impostor" is still a wonderful choice when you want a large, everblooming shrub. The loose growth habit of Cornelia makes it ideal for an informal landscape.

GARDEN PROFILE

The flowers are double, with 20–30 petals, and 1 inch wide; the color is medium pink with mauve and yellow tints. Fragrant blooms are produced in large clusters; they are just as beautiful in autumn as in summer. The glossy, bronze-green foliage readily complements the flowers. Moderately thorny, dark brown, arching canes are 6–8 feet long. Plants are disease resistant and winter hardy.

Gartendirektor Otto Linne (Shrub) Lambert, 193⁴

Gartendirektor Otto Linne bears a wealth of abundant blossoms on a small, bushy plant. It works well in the landscape when trained as a low-growing hedge.

GARDEN PROFILE

The double, deep pink flowers are 1½–2 inches wide, with 25–3⁵ petals. The midseason bloom is followed by a good repeat. Borne in clusters on 12-inch branches, the flowers have little or no fragrance. The spreading plants grow 3½–4½ feet tall, with smooth, nearly thornless canes. The light green to medium green leaves are semiglossy. Gartendirektor Otto Linne is disease resistant and winter hardy.

Hansa (Shrub)

Schaum & Van Tol, 1905

Intensely scented with the fragrance of cloves, Hansa belongs to the hybrid rugosa group of 20th-century shrub roses. Use it as a hedge or part of a shrub or mixed-flower border.

GARDEN PROFILE

The double, red-violet flowers are 3–3½ inches wide with 35–45 petals. Plants start blooming early in the season and continue throughout the summer into fall. The bloom form is rather loose and cupped. Large red hips, which are edible, ripen in the fall. The dense, bushy plants grow 5 feet tall. The very prickly canes bear dark green, deeply wrinkled foliage. Hansa is disease resistant and winter hardy. Prune plants periodically to encourage new growth and branching.

Frau Dagmar Hastrup (Shrub)   Unknown, c. 1914

This descendant of *Rosa rugosa* makes a superb low hedge. It is also a favorite haunt of bees in the garden. Many gardeners find that the repeat bloom in the fall is best. The hips, which follow flowers in the fall, can be harvested and made into preserves and other confections. Also called Frau Dagmar Hartopp.

GARDEN PROFILE

Clusters of bright, pointed buds open to saucer-shaped, 5-petaled flowers of clear, soft pink with golden stamens in the center and a strong scent of cloves. Blooms are 3–3½ inches across and borne from early in the season until frost. Hips ripen to bright red in the fall. Plants are dense and spreading, growing to 2½–3 feet tall and at least as wide. Canes are very thorny. The medium green leaves are deeply etched and wrinkled. This rose is disease free and winter hardy.

Marguerite Hilling (Shrub)

Hilling, 1959

Marguerite Hilling is a great addition to the garden—not only for its flowers, but also for its unusual red canes, which will enliven the gray landscape of winter. It is a pink sport, or mutation, of Nevada, seen opposite.

GARDEN PROFILE

The single, 5-petaled flowers, 4 inches wide, are at their showiest in midseason, but there is excellent repeat bloom. They are open and saucer shaped with little or no fragrance. Upright and arching, the practically thornless canes grow 6–8 feet tall. The leaves are small, gray-green, and semiglossy. Plants are disease resistant and reliably winter hardy.

Sparrieshoop (Shrub)

Kordes, 1953

Although introduced in recent years, Sparrieshoop captures the look of an old-fashioned single rose. The result of a cross between a floribunda and a sweetbrier rose, Sparrieshoop makes a beautiful accent plant in the landscape.

GARDEN PROFILE
The sweetly scented 4-inch-wide flowers open a rosy salmon-pink that fades to a pale pink. Flowers are borne in clusters. The center of each saucer-shaped flower is paler than the edges, and the stamens are yellow. Midseason bloom is very good, and it repeats fairly well. The very vigorous and bushy plants grow to 5 feet tall and not quite as wide. Young shoots and leaves are a deep copper-brown. As they mature, the glossy leaves turn a medium to deep green. Plants are disease resistant and winter hardy.

Belinda (Shrub)

Bentall, 1936

Belinda belongs to the hybrid musk group of shrub roses—big, blowsy plants that can be used as freestanding bushes or trained as low climbers. Even when planted in partial shade, some of the hybrid musk roses will manage a repeat bloom in fall. Belinda works particularly well as a hedge.

GARDEN PROFILE

The medium pink, semidouble flowers, with 12–15 petals, are just ¾ inch wide; they appear in clusters and give off a light fragrance. Blooms appear in midseason with a good repeat in fall. The plants are bushy, dense, and vigorous, growing up to 4–6 feet tall. The fairly smooth canes, with just a few thorns, have light green, semiglossy leaves. Belinda is disease resistant and winter hardy.

Pink Grootendorst (Shrub)

A Dutch hybrid, Pink Grootendorst is a color sport of the red hybrid rugosa F. J. Grootendorst. Both have frilly crimson flowers like a carnation's. Very tough and freely blooming, Pink Grootendorst is often used in hedges or borders.

GARDEN PROFILE

The flowers have a large midseason bloom, and the large clusters continue to be produced throughout the season. Each double pink flower is 1½ inches wide with 35–45 petals; there is no fragrance. The bushy and vigorous plants may reach 5–6 feet tall. Rather prickly, bristly stems bear semiglossy, wrinkled leaves of medium green. Disease resistant and winter hardy, Pink Grootendorst is amenable to pruning to almost any height above 3½ feet.

Constance Spry (Shrub)

Named for the English author, floral designer, and collector of old garden roses, Constance Spry is a modern shrub rose with the true old garden rose form. It can be grown as a loose, open shrub or trained on a wall or trellis.

GARDEN PROFILE

The very full, globular, light to medium pink flowers are 4½–5 inches wide, with 45–55 petals. They have a very fragrant, myrrhlike scent. Flowering is not recurrent, but there is a long period of midseason bloom. Blossoms appear individually along the branches. Growth is very strong and upright, with the moderately thorny canes arching gracefully. Plants will grow 5–6 feet tall. The gray to dark green leaves are semiglossy. Plants are disease resistant and winter hardy.

Will Scarlet (Shrub)

Hilling, 1948

A sport, or chance mutation, of a German-bred hybrid musk rose, Will Scarlet has become popular as a tall, impenetrable, everblooming hedge or screen. You might also consider it as a dazzling addition to the shrub border, as an accent plant, or even pruned as a pillar rose.

GARDEN PROFILE

Each brilliant red, semidouble flower is 3 inches wide with 24–30 petals. The fragrant, cup-shaped blooms are borne in clusters of 15–18. There is good repeat bloom after the first flowering of summer. At season's end, there are shiny orange hips that remain on the plants throughout the winter. Plants are upright, vigorous, and bushy. The moderately thorny canes grow 6 feet tall. Leaves are medium to dark green, or occasionally bronze-green. Will Scarlet is disease resistant and winter hardy.

Erfurt (Shrub)

Kordes, 1939

An intensely fragrant hybrid musk rose, Erfurt will work nicely as a bush or hedge plant. Like other members of its group, it has an arching habit, a characteristic that contributes to the abundance of blossoms it can produce.

GARDEN PROFILE

The flowers are semidouble, but look like single blooms; they have 10–15 petals. Lemon-white in the center with a broad pink edge, they open to 3½ inches wide and are saucer shaped. Erfurt blooms continuously throughout the season, bearing its flowers in clusters. The bushy, vigorous plants grow 5–6 feet tall. Canes are moderately thorny, with large, dark green, leathery, wrinkled leaves. Erfurt is disease resistant and winter hardy.

Alchymist (Shrub)

Kordes, 1956

The tall-growing Alchymist, with its unusually colored flowers, works well in the landscape as a large, open shrub; it is also excellent as a pillar rose or grown on a trellis.

GARDEN PROFILE

The apricot blend blossoms have the look of an old garden rose—very double, with 65–75 petals. Often, the petals form 4 sections in each flower. The fragrant blooms are 3½–4 inches across and appear from early season to midseason; the later flowers are slightly darker in color. Upright and vigorous, the plants grow 8–12 feet tall. The arching canes are very thorny and bear large, dark green, glossy leaves that sometimes appear coppery. Alchymist is disease resistant and winter hardy.

Margo Koster (Shrub)

Koster, 1931

Perhaps the most popular of the small-growing polyantha roses, Margo Koster is good for edgings, container plantings, mass plantings, or in mixed-flower plantings. It is especially attractive combined with blue flowers such as ageratum, Mealycup Sage, Love-in-a-Mist, or Balloon Flower. This rose has sported, or sent out chance mutations, numerous times; it is itself a sport of Dick Koster. There is a climbing form.

GARDEN PROFILE

The salmon-pink to coral, semidouble flowers are 1–1½ inches wide with 7–12 petals. Clusters of lightly fragrant, cup-shaped blooms are produced from midsummer until frost. Growing only 1 foot tall, this bushy, compact variety has very smooth, almost thornless canes with semiglossy, medium gray-green leaves. It is disease resistant and winter hardy.

Maigold (Shrub)

Kordes, 1953

A deep yellow shrub rose, Maigold is a superb choice for a border because of its bushy habit of growth.

GARDEN PROFILE

The deep yellow, semidouble flowers, with 14 petals, are 4 inches wide. They have a cupped form and a strong fragrance. The flowers appear from early in the season to midseason and do not repeat. The plants are upright, vigorous, and bushy. They bear medium green, glossy leaves, and grow to 5 feet tall. Maigold is disease resistant and reliably winter hardy.

Harison's Yellow (Shrub)

This popular shrub rose was a chance seedling. It is said to have been found in 1830 in the garden of a New York lawyer, whose country estate is now part of midtown Manhattan. A hardy, vigorous plant, Harison's Yellow was purportedly one of the plants often taken West by pioneers in covered wagons; folklore claims it as the "yellow rose of Texas." This adaptable rose is a good choice for the shrub border.

GARDEN PROFILE

The deep yellow, semidouble flowers are 2–2½ inches wide with 20–24 petals. Sweetly scented, they bloom very early in the season and do not repeat. The cupped blooms surround showy golden stamens. Flowers occur along the entire length of the arching, dark mahogany-brown, very thorny canes. The fernlike leaves are small, abundant, and light to medium green. Growing 5–7 feet tall, the upright, spreading bush is very vigorous. Disease resistant and winter hardy.

Zéphirine Drouhin (Old Garden)

Bizot, 1868

The best known and best loved of all the Bourbon roses, Zéphirine Drouhin is the only variety that the hybridizer Bizot is known to have produced. An excellent low to medium climber, it is recommended for areas near walkways because of its fragrance and its nearly thornless canes. It may also be used as a large shrub, and its size kept in check with pruning. In the garden, Zéphirine Drouhin is sensational in beds or borders of pink flowers.

Garden Profile

The semidouble, deep cerise pink flowers, with perhaps 20–24 petals, are 3½–4 inches wide and have a raspberrylike fragrance. Flowers hold their color well until they drop cleanly. Abundant clusters of loose, cup-shaped flowers are produced from early summer almost continuously until frost. Upright, vigorous, and well branched, the canes are very smooth and grow 8–12 feet tall. New growth is red-bronze, changing to a semiglossy green. Winter hardy; mildew and black spot may be a problem in humid climates.

This is the Apothecary Rose, probably the most famous rose of all time. First recorded in the 13th century, it was possibly brought to France from Damascus by a Crusader. For several centuries it was the mainstay of a flourishing industry centered around the French town of Provins. Fashioned into preserves, syrups, and powders, it was believed to cure many and diverse ailments.

GARDEN PROFILE

The deep pink, semidouble flowers have 12–18 petals; these are fragrant when fresh but even more so when dried. The cupped blossoms, 3–3½ inches wide, open to reveal golden stamens. Blooming in midsummer, they do not repeat. Attractive, round, red hips ripen later in the season. Plants are rounded and compact. The upright canes grow 3–3½ feet tall. The canes have few thorns, but they are bristly. The medium-sized leaves are roughly textured and medium green. Disease resistant and winter hardy.

Königin von Dänemark (Old Garden)

On its introduction, the alba "Queen of Denmark" was considered the perfection of form. It is still popular today. Königin von Dänemark works as a freestanding shrub, or trained against a wall. Like other albas, it will grow and bloom in partial shade as well as sun.

GARDEN PROFILE

As the beautifully shaped buds begin to open, the flower is an intense carmine color. This shade remains at the center as the flowers open to a soft, light pink. Upon full expansion, the outer petals reflex and fade to nearly white. The very double flowers, 3½ inches wide, may have as many as 200 petals; the bloom divides into quarters, with a button eye in the center. The fragrance is very intense and sweet. Bloom is early in the season, with no repeat. Upright, treelike plants grow to 6 feet tall. The canes are very thorny, with rough, dull, blue-green leaves, darker than those of most albas. This rose is disease free and winter hardy.

Believed to be the same as Parsons' Pink China Rose, this rose from China has been grown in the western world since the mid- to late 1700s. Old Blush and its descendants have been used in hybridization work through the years, contributing the characteristic of continual flowering to our present-day roses.

GARDEN PROFILE

The double flowers, with perhaps 24–30 petals, are silvery pink and 3 inches wide. The color deepens slightly as the blooms age. With a light fragrance reminiscent of sweet peas, the loose, cupped flowers are produced from early summer until mid-fall in clusters. Growing 3–4 feet tall, Old Blush forms moderately vigorous, bushy, upright plants. The canes are smooth, with few thorns. The leaves are smooth, medium green, and glossy. A highly adaptable plant that withstands a certain amount of neglect, Old Blush is disease resistant, but it is not winter hardy. Grow it as a small bush in a border, as a hedge, or train on a wall.

Henri Martin (Old Garden)

Laffay, 186?

This is a centifolia moss—that is, a rose that has sported from a centifolia rose and bears mossy growth on the buds. The elegant Henri Martin produces great quantities of flowers.

GARDEN PROFILE

Dark crimson fading to a deep rose, the double blooms are 2½ inches wide with perhaps 65–75 rounded, flat petals. Fragrant and camellia-like, the well-shaped blooms appear in clusters in midseason to late season but do not repeat. There is green moss on the buds. Plants grow 5 feet tall; they are upright, vigorous, and bushy. The thorny canes bear lush foliage that is medium to dark green and rough. Disease resistant and winter hardy.

William Lobb (Old Garden)

Laffay, 1855

Also called the Old Velvet Moss, William Lobb has very mossy buds that give off a strong pine scent when touched. Yellow- or cream-colored border plants provide a lovely contrast to this rose.

GARDEN PROFILE

The flowers are deep mauve with pale lavender on the reverse; they fade to a slate-purple. Blooms are double, with 65–75 petals, and 3 inches wide; they are very fragrant and the large outer petals enclose many shorter central petals. The large flower clusters appear in mid-summer, with no repeat. The vigorous, open, upright plants grow 4–5 feet tall. The strong canes are bristly and thorny. The leaves are a soft medium green. Plants are winter hardy and disease resistant, although somewhat susceptible to mildew. They may need support.

Rose du Roi (Old Garden)

Descended from the earliest Portland rose, Rose du Roi was raised in the king's garden at Sèvres in 1815. This red rose and its purple sport, Rose du Roi à Fleurs Pourprés, were a sensation in their day. The deepest shadings occur on the outer petals and the top surface.

GARDEN PROFILE
The very fragrant flowers are double, with perhaps 100 petals, and 2½ inches wide. The large outer petals surround short central petals. Blooms appear in midseason; flowering continues until frost. The vigorous and compact plants grow 3–4 feet tall. Canes are moderately thorny, and the leaves are a semi-glossy medium green. Rose du Roi is disease resistant and winter hardy.

Belle de Crècy (Old Garden)

Rose lore has it that this gallica was named for Madame de Pompadour and grown in the garden at her estate at Crècy. It is perhaps more likely that the name was considered appropriate for a rose from a nursery in the area. Often stunning, Belle de Crècy works best grown with white-flowering plants.

GARDEN PROFILE

The fragrant flowers are 2½–3 inches wide and very double. The violet tones develop quickly, so blooms of pink and shades of mauve, lavender, or gray occur at the same time. The evenly petaled blooms have a green button center. Petals reflex into a ball when fully open. Plants flower for a longer period in summer but do not repeat. The rounded, compact bushes grow 3½–4½ feet tall. Canes are bristly rather than thorny. The leaves have a tough, dull texture. The plants are disease resistant and winter hardy, but mildew may be a problem in some areas, especially the South. Canes tend to be somewhat lax; some staking or the use of a support is advisable.

Tuscany (Old Garden)

Also known as the Old Velvet Rose, for the color and texture of the blossoms, Tuscany is probably the same as Gerard's Velvet Rose, which was described in 1596. Tuscany is considered one of the best of the gallica roses. It combines well with other old roses with intense color—such as Variegata di Bologna, Roger Lambelin, and Grüss an Teplitz—and gray-leaved plants like Dusty Miller, lavender, pinks, rosemary, and sage.

GARDEN PROFILE

The intensely dark flowers may take on a purple, maroon-crimson, dark red, or brown-crimson hue. The semidouble flowers, with 18–24 petals, are 3–3½ inches wide; these very fragrant, rather loose, cupped blooms show bright golden stamens in the center. Plants bloom in mid-summer with no repeat. Rounded and compact bushes grow 3–4 feet tall, with upright, bristly canes. The small, rough leaves are medium to dark green. Tuscany is disease resistant and winter hardy.

Nuits de Young (Old Garden)

Laffay, 1845

Another moss rose produced by the Frenchman Laffay, this dark, dusky rose was named for the 18th-century English poet Edward Young. His 9-volume poem, *The Complaint; or Night-Thoughts on Life, Death, and Immortality*—commonly referred to as *Night Thoughts*—gave rise to the "graveyard school" of poetry. Nuits de Young works well in a shrub or flower border, grown with contrasting yellow-flowering plants.

Garden Profile

Flowers are dark maroon with purple; they are double, with perhaps 50 petals, and very fragrant, opening to 2½ inches wide. Fading very little as they age, the dark, velvety blooms are highlighted with a few golden stamens in the center. Flowering is in midsummer, with no repeat. With thin, open growth, the thorny canes grow 5 feet tall. The sparse foliage is small and dark, overlaid with a hint of maroon. Nuits de Young is disease resistant and winter hardy.

Tour de Malakoff (Old Garden) Soupert & Notting, 1856

One of the most unusually colored of all roses, this centifolia may be grown with support as a pillar rose. An English method of growing is to arch the branches over and peg them with forked sticks; blooms then appear along the length of the canes. Combine this rose with silver-foliaged plants and fuchsias of a complementary color.

GARDEN PROFILE

The deep mauve to carmine-purple flowers are loosely double, with perhaps 45–55 petals, and grow to 3–3½ inches across. As they fade, their color changes to a violet or gray-blue. The veins in the thin petals are very pronounced, and the center is green. This fragrant rose blooms profusely at midseason. Growth is upright, vigorous, and sprawling. Canes grow 6–7 feet tall and are very thorny. The leaves are a medium to dark green. Plants are disease free and winter hardy.

Cardinal de Richelieu (Old Garden) Laffay, 1840

This rose's blooms are the deepest in color of all the gallica roses. On an overcast day, very deep midnight blue tones are prevalent; on sunny days, the flower is a rich purple. Some authorities point to a possible China rose influence in this variety. Whatever the source, it is one of the most famous varieties. Garden expert Graham Stuart Thomas recommends growing it with Celeste and Maiden's Blush, while Peter Malins, another authority, suggests candy-pink moss roses as companions.

GARDEN PROFILE

The sweetly fragrant, loosely cupped flowers are double, with perhaps 35–45 velvety petals, and 2½–3 inches wide. Blooming in clusters in midsummer, the flowers do not recur. Upright plants grow to a compact 2½–3 feet tall; they are often dense. The thin canes bear small, dark green, semiglossy leaves and very few thorns. Disease resistant and winter hardy, Cardinal de Richelieu needs the very best of soil, water, and fertilizer.

Reine des Violettes (Old Garden)   Millet-Malet, 1860

This is one of the most highly valued of the hybrid perpetuals; rose specialists from around the world consider it the epitome of the old rose. The flowers present a changing blend of lavender, sometimes with tones very much on the blue side of mauve.

GARDEN PROFILE

Quite double, with perhaps 75 petals, the cupped, muddled flowers are intensely fragrant. Each bloom is about 3 inches wide; the bushes are profusely covered in midsummer, then bear occasional flowers the rest of the season. Vigorous, bushy, and rounded, Reine des Violettes grows 5–6 feet tall. The canes are very smooth, with few thorns. The soft leaves, abundantly produced, are a medium green. The foliage is reported to have a pepper-like fragrance, but this is usually difficult to detect. Reine des Violettes is disease resistant and winter hardy. It needs to be grown in rich soil, and fed and watered well.

Paul Neyron (Old Garden)

This 19th-century hybrid perpetual is fabled for the size of its blooms, which can reach 6–7 inches on occasion. They are excellent as cut flowers, somewhat resembling peonies. The bloom color does not fade with age.

GARDEN PROFILE

The very double, deep pink flowers are usually 4½–5½ inches wide, with 65–75 petals; the somewhat fragrant, globe- to cup-shaped blooms are tightly packed with petals. Bloom is in midsummer, with fall repeat. The upright and vigorous plants, with arching canes, grow to 5–6 feet tall. The canes are fairly smooth, with few thorns. The large leaves are medium green and semiglossy. Plants are disease resistant and winter hardy. Arch the branches over and stake them about 2 feet above the ground; they will send out flowering shoots all along the canes.

OLD-FASHIONED ROSES **77**

Ferdinand Pichard (Old Garden)

Tanne, 1921

Among striped roses, Ferdinand Pichard ranks with Rosa Mundi for startling effect. A hybrid perpetual, it is quite similar to the Bourbon rose Commandant Beaurepaire, although no record of parentage links the two.

GARDEN PROFILE

The flowers are double, with 25 petals, and 3 inches wide. On opening, they are a clear pink marked with crimson; as they age, they become blush marked with purple. The cupped blooms are fragrant. A good midsummer bloom is followed by intermittent flowering the rest of the season. The moderately vigorous and compact plants grow 4–5 feet tall. The upright canes are fairly smooth, with few thorns. The long, pointed leaves, light to medium green, have a soft texture. Plants are disease resistant and winter hardy. If you arch the branches well over and tie them to stakes, you will have flowering shoots along the entire length of the canes.

Commandant Beaurepaire

Moreau-Robert, 1874
(Old Garden)

This spectacular striped Bourbon rose is also known as Panachée d'Angers. It is unusual because its variously colored stripes and splashes appear on deep pink petals, rather than on a paler background. A supposed sport, or mutation, called Honorine de Brabant has colorful stripes against a paler pink background.

GARDEN PROFILE

Flowers are double, with perhaps 35–45 petals; they are fragrant and grow to 3–3½ inches wide. Bloom is mainly in midseason, with a very sparse repeat. The long, pointed, wavy leaves are a light yellow-green. Growing 4–5 feet tall, the smooth, almost thornless canes are upright and vigorous. Plants are disease resistant and winter hardy; mildew may be a problem in humid climates. Prune older canes to keep the plant from becoming overgrown; pruning after the first flowering will encourage repeat blooms.

Rosa Mundi (Old Garden)

This striking sport of *Rosa gallica officinalis* is the earliest-known striped rose. Legend has it that Rosa Mundi takes its name from an association with the Fair Rosamund, mistress of Henry II of England. In today's world, it works well in a mixed shrub or flower border, or as a low hedge.

GARDEN PROFILE

The fragrant flowers are medium pink to deep pink, striped with blush or white and centered with golden stamens. Semidouble, with 18–24 petals, the cupped blooms are 3–3½ inches wide. Flowers are produced in midsummer with no repeat. Round red hips appear later. Plants are rounded and compact. The upright, bristly canes grow 3–3½ feet tall; the leaves are rough and medium green. Rosa Mundi is disease resistant and winter hardy; it grows best only after it becomes well established. It responds well to humus-rich soil, plenty of water, and fertilizer. Remove bare or thin canes, and any branches with solid-colored blooms, after flowering.

Camaieux (Old Garden)

This rose not only has stripes, but has stripes that change color! At first, the background is white, with the stripes and splashes a light red. This quickly changes to violet, then magenta, and finally a pale lavender gray. Camaieux is considered one of the best of the striped roses. It combines well with Belle de Crècy and Madame Hardy.

GARDEN PROFILE

The fragrant double blooms, with perhaps 65 petals, are 3–3½ inches wide. The petals are rather loosely arranged, forming a shape variously described as cupped or camellialike. Golden stamens sometimes show at the center. Flowers are produced from early summer to midsummer with no repeat; hips appear later in the season. The plants are rounded and compact, with flexible, arching branches; they grow to 3–3½ feet tall. The bristly canes, with few thorns, bear medium gray-green leaves. Camaieux is winter hardy and disease resistant, but prone to mildew in the South.

Général Kléber (Old Garden)

Robert, 1856

Most moss roses have rather rangy, gaunt-looking canes, but Général Kléber has a dense habit of growth. It commemorates the general whom Napoleon selected to look after his army in Egypt; he is reported to have been a very kind man, and much loved by his troops.

GARDEN PROFILE

Flowers are double, with perhaps 100 petals, and 2½–3 inches across. The very fragrant blossoms may be quartered or crumpled, with a button center. The clusters are accented with mossy buds and stems. Bloom is at midseason, with no repeat. The upright, vigorous, bushy plants grow 5 feet tall; canes are sometimes thorny. The large, lush leaves are a fresh green. Plants are disease resistant and winter hardy.

Louise Odier (Old Garden)

Considering that it only has 35–45 petals, the blossoms of Louise Odier, displaying classic old-rose form, appear very full. Gardeners often combine this Bourbon rose with 2 others of similar form, La Reine Victoria and Madame Pierre Oger.

GARDEN PROFILE

This rose produces abundant clusters of flowers at midseason, followed by good repeat bloom. Each medium pink, fragrant flower is about 3½ inches across. The bush is more slender and upright than is the rule for the big, blowsy Bourbons. Plants typically grow 4½–5½ feet tall. The canes are smooth with few thorns, and the leaves are light to medium green. Louise Odier is winter hardy and generally disease resistant, although it may be susceptible to mildew in humid climates. Fertilize and water plants well to encourage autumn flowering; prune after the first summer bloom period.

Celsiana (Old Garden)

Depicted by the artists Van Huysum and Redouté, Celsiana was first grown in Holland and later introduced into France by a rose breeder named Cels. This lovely old-fashioned rose may be the quintessential damask. Its blossoms are imbued with the intense fragrance of attar of roses.

GARDEN PROFILE

Many flowers are produced during the long midsummer blooming period. Emerging from dark buds, the light pink, semidouble flowers are 3½–4 inches wide, with 12–18 silken, folded petals. The blooms open to a wide, cupped form, showing golden stamens. As they age, the flowers fade to a blush pink. A few tubular red hips ripen later. The plants form an upright, vigorous, open clump of moderately thorny canes, 3½–4 feet tall. The light gray-green leaves have a soft, dull finish. Celsiana is disease free and winter hardy.

Crested Moss (Old Garden)

Vibert, 1827

Also known as Chapeau de Napoléon and *Rosa centifolia cristata,* this rose bears just a fringe of sparse brownish moss on the edges of the sepals. This fringe gives the buds the appearance of a tricornered hat. Most likely a chance seedling, it is reputed to have been found growing in a convent wall at Fribourg, Switzerland, in 1820.

GARDEN PROFILE

The flowers are medium pink and very double, with perhaps 200 petals, and almost globelike. They are 3–3½ inches wide and quite fragrant. The plants produce clusters of flowers once in midseason and do not repeat. Plants have a very open habit. The upright, vigorous, arching canes grow 5–7 feet tall. The very bristly and thorny canes bear rough, dull, medium green leaves. Plants are winter hardy and disease resistant, although mildew and black spot may appear. This rose should be well fertilized and watered. It can withstand hard pruning. Some support or staking may be necessary.

Fantin-Latour (Old Garden)

Although classified as a centifolia, this beautiful rose does not really fit into the centifolia class, for it has few thorns and a bushy habit. Named after a celebrated French floral painter of the 19th century, this rose is one of the most handsome of the old garden roses.

GARDEN PROFILE

The pale blush flowers are double, with perhaps 200 petals, and 3–3½ inches wide. Borne in large clusters, these blooms do not recur but they are produced over a relatively long period in midsummer. Very fragrant, they are at first cup shaped, then open with the petals flat or somewhat reflexed. There is often a green "button" in the center. The plants are upright, vigorous, and well branched, growing 5–6 feet tall and as wide. The canes have few thorns. Leaves are smooth, medium green, and semiglossy. Fantin-Latour is disease resistant and winter hardy.

Petite de Hollande (Old Garden)

This small centifolia is considered to be the best of the Provence roses for smaller gardens. It is also known by the names Pompon des Dames, Petite Junon de Hollande, and Normandica.

GARDEN PROFILE

The soft, clear pink flowers with a darker center are very full and globular; 2–2½ inches wide, they are double, with 45–55 petals. The fragrant flowers are held erect in small clusters. The blooming period is very long during midsummer, but it does not repeat. The upright, vigorous, and bushy plants grow 3½–4 feet tall. The canes are very thorny. The leaves are small, deeply toothed, and a fresh green color. Petite de Hollande is winter hardy and disease resistant, except for a slight tendency to mildew.

Gloire de Guilan (Old Garden)

Hilling, 1949

Arather exotic damask, Gloire de Guilan was discovered in the Caspian provinces of Persia by Miss Nancy Lindsay. Descendants of *Rosa damascena,* the damasks—along with the gallicas—are among the most ancient of cultivated roses. In the days of the Roman Empire, damask roses were grown in heated houses so that they would bloom out of season; they were known throughout the empire, and were preserved from extinction during the Middle Ages in the gardens of monastaries.

GARDEN PROFILE

The light pink, double flowers of this damask, 3 inches wide, have 45–55 petals. Intensely fragrant, the flowers bloom profusely early in the season, with no repeat. The open flower has a full, globular form with a quartered center. The plants are vigorous but somewhat sprawling; they grow to 3–5 feet tall. The canes are moderately thorny, clothed in soft, dull, light green leaves. Gloire de Guilan is disease free and winter hardy.

Belle Isis (Old Garden)

Thﬁs delicate pink hybrid was introduced in the same year that the wild *Rosa rugosa* first made its appearance on the North American continent. Belle Isis is a gallica rose, descended from the roses cultivated and distributed around Europe by the Romans. Like other gallicas, Belle Isis is a tidy, neat, upright rose that holds its pretty blooms poised aloft.

GARDEN PROFILE

The light pink flowers, 2½–3 inches wide, are double, with perhaps 45–55 petals. The blossoms are fragrant, cupped, and packed tightly with petals. Belle Isis blooms in midseason with no repeat. The plants are compact, rounded, and bushy, growing to 2½–3 feet tall. The canes are bristly but not thorny, with small, gray-green leaves. This rose is disease resistant and winter hardy.

Comte de Chambord

A Portland, or damask perpetual, rose, Comte de Chambord is an excellent plant for the front of a shrub border or planted in a mixed flower border, particularly one devoted to shades of pink.

GARDEN PROFILE

The very full, rose-pink to mauve-tinted blossoms, with perhaps 200 petals, are 3 inches wide. The full outer petals enclose many central petals. Blooms are sometimes quartered, reflexing when fully expanded. With a rich, heady fragrance, the flowers are produced from midsummer until frost. The rounded and compact bushes grow 3½–4 feet tall. The sturdy, moderately thorny canes bear large, semi-glossy, light to medium green leaves. Comte de Chambord is disease resistant and winter hardy.

Gloire des Mousseuses (Old Garden) Laffay, 1852

This centifolia moss has very large blooms for its class, with some 5 inches wide. The name may be alternately spelled as Mousseaux or Mousseux.

GARDEN PROFILE
Light to medium pink with a faint lavender tint, the flowers are very double, with perhaps 200 petals. Quartered, with a button center, they are quite fragrant and long lasting. Plants bloom in midsummer, with no repeat. Growing 3–4 feet tall, plants form a stiffly upright, compact, moderately vigorous bush. Canes are very thorny, and the buds and stems have heavy mossing. The leaves are soft, dull, and light green. Gloire des Mousseuses is disease resistant and winter hardy.

Stanwell Perpetual (Old Garden)

Lee, 1838

Believed to be a cross between *Rosa damascena semperflorens* and *Rosa spinosissima,* this is the only spinosissima hybrid that is a reliable repeat bloomer. A gracefully arching shrub, its long flowering season makes it an excellent and reliable choice for a hedge or addition to the shrub border.

GARDEN PROFILE

Light pink fading to white, the fragrant double flowers are 3–3½ inches wide with perhaps 45–55 petals. The blooms appear singly on very short stems from early summer to midsummer. The loose, muddled form of the flowers gives an even appearance. Vigorous and spreading plants grow 3–5 feet tall and as wide. The canes are very thorny. The small, dull leaves are blue-green to deep green. Plants are disease resistant and winter hardy. Prune the oldest growth out each season, as younger growth produces better flowers and foliage. Only well-established plants have a reliable repeat bloom.

Souvenir de la Malmaison

Beluse, 1843
(Old Garden)

The rose garden maintained by the Empress Josephine, first wife of Napoleon Bonaparte, is considered to have been the first international rose collection. In the fabulous grounds of Malmaison, Josephine's residence outside of Paris, 250 varieties of roses were grown. Named in honor of the garden, Souvenir de la Malmaison is an unforgettable rose, but unfortunately a very sparse bloomer. Use it near the front of a rose or shrub border, or as part of a perennial border. There is a climbing form.

GARDEN PROFILE

Each light pink, 4½- to 5-inch bloom is very double, with 65–75 petals and a strong spicy fragrance. The blooms are usually quartered (with the petals divided into sections). Bloom begins in midseason or later; a few flowers appear in fall. The moderately thorny canes grow only 2–3 feet tall, but the bushes are vigorous. Leaves are medium green and semiglossy. Disease resistant and winter hardy with some protection. Mildew may be a problem in humid climates.

Maiden's Blush (Old Garden)

Before 1600

This alba's long history probably accounts for the many names it has been given: Great Maiden's Blush, La Virginale, La Séduisante, La Royale, Incarnata, and Cuisse de Nymphe; when deeper color develops, the rose is sometimes called Cuisse de Nymphe Emué. No matter what you call it, Maiden's Blush works well as an informal hedge or as part of a shrub border.

GARDEN PROFILE

Produced in clusters, the very fragrant, light blush-pink flowers are 2½–3 inches wide and very double, with over 200 petals. Most of the time the centers are muddled, but under good cultivation a button center will occasionally develop. The bloom is extremely profuse from early season to midseason but does not recur. Young plants are stiffly upright, eventually arching out; they grow to 5–6 feet tall. The canes are very bristly and thorny, with rough, dull, blue-green leaves. Disease free and winter hardy.

Alfred de Dalmas (Old Garden)

Portemer, 1855

Also known as Mousseline, this delicately colored moss rose probably has damask and Portland roses in its heritage. It is a superlative plant for the landscape. Grow it in a rose garden, mixed flower border, as a mass planting, or even in containers outdoors.

GARDEN PROFILE

Light blush pink fading to white, the fragrant, cupped flowers are 2½–3 inches wide; double, with 55–65 petals. A sparse, brownish moss marks the calyx surrounding the buds as well as the stems. Blooms are produced in clusters during midsummer, and then intermittently throughout the season. The bushy, spreading plants grow 2½–3 feet tall. The very bristly canes bear rough, gray-green leaves. Disease resistant and winter hardy.

Félicité et Perpétue (Old Garden) Jacques, 1827

Bred by the gardener to the Duc d'Orleans, this hybrid sempervirens is a rampant-growing, nearly indestructible plant in mild climates, where it is almost evergreen. Use it as a large bush or train it up and over a wall.

GARDEN PROFILE

The creamy white double flowers, 1½ inches wide with about 65 petals, are delicately fragrant. These full, globe-shaped blooms are borne in large clusters that completely cover the plant at the height of summer. Very vigorous, it will grow 20 feet tall. The abundant, small, glossy leaves are maroon when young, turning green. Plants are disease free but not winter hardy. Pruning is not advised.

Champneys' Pink Cluster

The forerunner of the Noisette class, Champneys' Pink Cluster was an American invention, the result of crossing China and musk roses. It was produced by John Champneys, a wealthy owner of rice plantations in Charleston, South Carolina. Introduced at the beginning of the 19th century, it was used by Philippe Noisette, a Charleston florist, in further hybridization work. His roses as well as other hybrids were to bear his name.

GARDEN PROFILE

Blush to deep pink, the double flowers have 24 petals and are 2 inches wide. The very fragrant cupped flowers are borne in clusters. Bloom begins in midseason, continuing until frost. The upright, vigorous, arching canes grow 8–12 feet tall. Canes are very smooth, with few thorns, and the leaves are a glossy medium green. Plants are disease resistant but not winter hardy except in milder climates.

Leda (Old Garden)

This rose is also called the Painted Damask, because its white petals look as if the tips have been daubed with red paint. Leda's lax habit can be a challenge to gardeners. It should be trained upright to a low trellis or other support.

GARDEN PROFILE

Flowers are very double, with perhaps 200 petals, and 2½–3 inches wide. They open from fat, red-brown buds into reflexed balls. The blooms are fragrant, with many having a button eye; they appear in midseason with no repeat. The trailing, thorny canes will grow to 2½–3 feet tall if trained upright. Leaves are rounded and a dark gray-green. Disease free and winter hardy.

Mabel Morrison (Old Garden)

Broughton, 1878

This hybrid perpetual has been compared to the Portlands because its blooms have short stems and seem to nestle among the foliage. It is a sport, or mutation, of Baroness Rothschild.

GARDEN PROFILE

The flowers are white, blushed with pink; this coloration is more intense in the fall repeat bloom. The double flowers, with 30 petals, are 3½–4 inches wide and fragrant. The upright, vigorous, and well-branched plants grow 4–4½ feet tall. The canes are moderately thorny. The semiglossy leaves are medium green to dark gray-green. Mabel Morrison is disease resistant and winter hardy.

Madame Hardy (Old Garden)

Described as sumptuous, elegant, unsurpassable, and even ravishing, Madame Hardy is considered to be among the very finest of the full-petaled damask roses, and it is perhaps the most popular white rose of its type. It was created by the superintendent of the Luxembourg Gardens in Paris, and named for his wife. It blooms only once a season—but how much can one ask of such beauty?

Garden Profile

The very double flowers, with perhaps 200 petals, are usually 3–3½ inches wide; the fragrant blooms appear in midsummer and exhibit a button eye. Flowers open to a cup shape, then become flat, with the outermost petals curving backward. The upright, vigorous, bushy plants grow 5–5½ feet tall, with moderately thorny canes. The abundant leaves are a fresh-looking bright or dark green. Disease free and winter hardy, the plants may need to be staked or have the canes tied together about halfway up.

Frau Karl Druschki (Old Garden)   Lambert, 1901

This white hybrid perpetual is also called Reine des Neiges, Snow Queen, and White American Beauty. Its fine form and reliability have made it one of the most popular of the older white roses. The long, strong stems make it ideal for cutting. This is a large plant, so place it near the back of a border, train it along a fence, or grow it as a pillar rose. The white flowers are best shown off against a dark green hedge. There is a climbing form.

GARDEN PROFILE

The double flowers, with 35 petals, are 4–4½ inches wide and have a high-centered form. Most of the scentless flowers are produced in midsummer, with good repeat throughout the rest of the season. The upright, vigorous, and well-branched plants grow 5–7 feet tall. Canes are fairly smooth with few thorns; the large, plentiful leaves are medium green. Frau Karl Druschki is disease resistant and winter hardy; flowers have a tendency to ball in hot, rainy weather.

Madame Legras de St. Germain

1846

(Old Garden

Thought to be an alba crossed with a damask, Madame Legras de St. Germain is a lovely addition to an all-white garden of shrubs, perennials, and annuals. Its lustrous, delicate-looking white blooms are fortunately tougher than they appear, and they are not easily spoiled by rain.

GARDEN PROFILE

The very double white blooms with a lemon-yellow center are 3½ inches wide with 200 petals. Produced in large clusters, they are sweetly fragrant. They bloom once each year, early in the season. Upon fully opening, the tightly packed petals reflex into a ball. Plants will reach 6–7 feet tall when grown as a shrub; with support, they will grow to about twice that height. The thin, arching canes are nearly thornless, with light to medium green leaves. Disease free and winter hardy.

102 OLD-FASHIONED ROSES

Sombreuil (Old Garden)

Robert, 1850

A climbing tea rose, Sombreuil is well worth trying in protected positions in northern gardens. It is sometimes referred to as a refined Souvenir de la Malmaison, because of its flat, quartered flowers. Although usually grown as a climber, it can also be allowed to develop as a dense shrub.

GARDEN PROFILE

The flowers are a creamy white and very double, with perhaps 100 petals. The fragrance is a strong classic-tea scent. Each flower is about 3½–4 inches wide. Blooms are produced throughout the summer. The upright, vigorous, moderately thorny canes grow 12–15 feet tall. The leathery, semiglossy leaves are medium green. Sombreuil is disease resistant and borderline winter hardy. In the North, plant it in the warmest, least exposed site in your garden and be sure to provide plenty of winter protection.

Celine Forestier (Old Garden)

Trouillard, 1842

Celine Forestier was a later development of the Noisette group of roses, bringing yellow into the class. This rose makes an excellent small climber.

GARDEN PROFILE

The yellow flowers, sometimes with a tinge of pink or peach, are double, with 24 petals, and 2–2½ inches wide. Bloom starts in midseason and the plants are seldom out of flower until fall. The very fragrant cupped blossoms occur in clusters. The upright, vigorous, arching canes reach 10–15 feet tall. The canes are fairly smooth with few thorns, and the leaves are medium green and semiglossy. Celine Forestier is disease free but not winter hardy. It is a slow grower, requiring rich soil.

APPENDICES

Map: Paul Singer

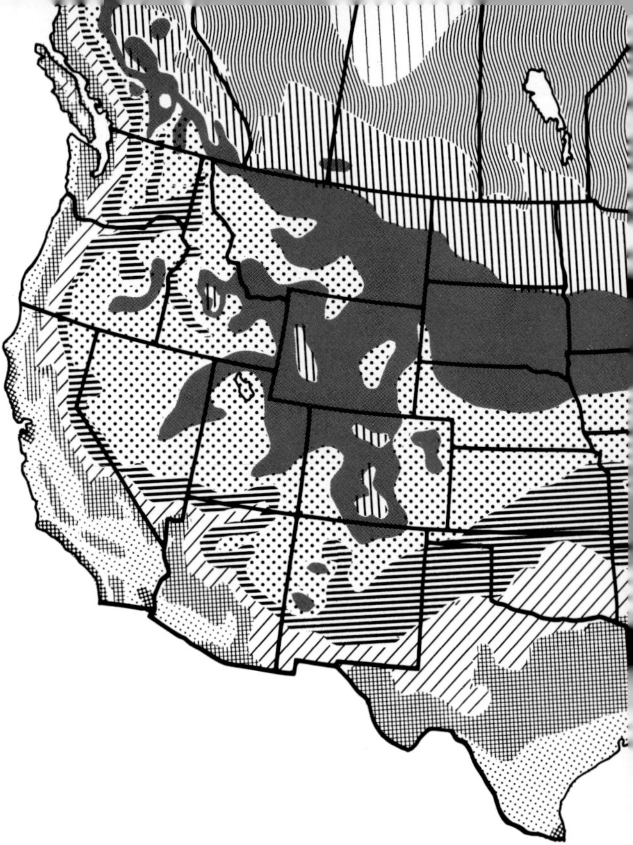

HARDINESS ZONE MAP

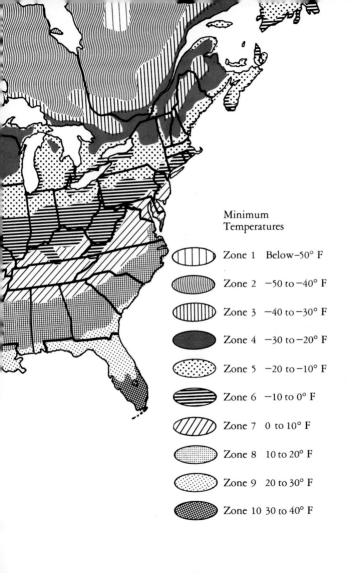

Minimum
Temperatures

Zone 1   Below −50° F

Zone 2   −50 to −40° F

Zone 3   −40 to −30° F

Zone 4   −30 to −20° F

Zone 5   −20 to −10° F

Zone 6   −10 to 0° F

Zone 7   0 to 10° F

Zone 8   10 to 20° F

Zone 9   20 to 30° F

Zone 10 30 to 40° F

GARDEN PESTS AND DISEASES

PLANT DISEASES, insects, and other pests are a fact of life for a gardener. No matter what you grow or how large your garden, it is helpful to become familiar with the common problems in your area and to learn how to control them. Since the general symptoms of plant problems—yellowing of leaves, death or disappearance of plant parts, stunting, poor growth, and wilting—can be caused by a multitude of diseases or pests, some experience is needed to determine which culprit is attacking your roses.

Diseases

Fungi and bacteria cause a variety of diseases, ranging from leaf spots and wilts to root rot, but bacterial diseases usually make the affected plant tissues appear wetter than fungi do. Viruses and mycoplasma are microorganisms too small to be seen with an ordinary microscope. They are often transmitted by insects, such as aphids and leafhoppers, and cause mottled yellow or deformed leaves and stunted growth. Nematodes are microscopic roundworms that usually live in association with plant roots; they cause stunting and poor growth, and sometimes produce galls on leaves. The way a particular disease organism has spread to your roses influences the control measures you may need to take.

Insects and Other Pests

Roses attract many different kinds of insects. Sap-sucking insects—including aphids, leafhoppers, and scale insects—suck plant juices, leaving the victim yellow, stunted, and misshapen. They also produce honeydew, a sticky substance that attracts ants and sooty mold fungus. Thrips and spider mites scrape plant tissue and suck the juices that well up in the injured areas. Beetles and caterpillars consume leaves, whole or in part. Borers tunnel into shoots and stems, where they deposit their eggs; the larvae that hatch feed on plant tissue. Some insects, such as grubs and maggots, are rarely seen above ground. They are destructive nonetheless, because they feed on roots, weakening or killing the plant.

Environmental Stresses

Some plant injuries are caused by severe weather conditions, salt toxicity, rodents, nutritional deficiencies or excesses, pesticides, or damage from lawn mowers. You can avoid many of these injuries by being aware of potential dangers and taking proper precautions.

Methods of Control

Controlling plant pests and diseases is not as overwhelming a task as it may seem. Many of the measures, performed on a day-to-day basis, are preventive, so that you don't have to rely on pesticides that may not be very effective once a culprit has attacked your roses. Observe plants each week for signs of trouble. That way you can prevent or limit a disease or infestation in the early stages.

Your normal gardening routine should include preventive measures. By cultivating the soil regularly, you expose insect and disease-causing organisms to the sun and thus lessen their chances of survival. In the fall, destroy infested and diseased canes, remove dead leaves and flowers, and clean up plant debris. Do not add diseased or infested material to the compost pile. Spray plants with water to dislodge insects and remove suffocating dust. Pick off larger insects by hand. To discourage fungal leaf spots and blights, water plants in the morning and allow leaves to dry off before nightfall. For the same reason, provide adequate air circulation around leaves and stems by giving plants sufficient space.

Always buy healthy, certified, disease-free plants. Check leaves and canes for dead areas and for off-color and stunted tissue. Make sure that your roses are properly cared for.

Insecticides and Fungicides

Weeds provide a home for insects and diseases, so pull them up or use herbicides. Be careful near roses, however, since they are very sensitive to weed-killers. Herbicide injury may cause elongated, straplike, or downward-cupping leaves. Do not apply herbicides, including "weed-and-feed" lawn preparations, too close to flower beds. Spray weed-killers only when there is little air movement, but not on a very hot, dry day.

To protect plant tissue from damage done by insects and diseases, you may choose from among the many insecticides and fungicides that are available. Few products, however, can control diseases that result from bacteria, viruses, and mycoplasma.

Pesticides are usually either "protectant" or "systemic" in nature. Protectants ward off insects or disease organisms from uninfected foliage, while systemics can move through the plant and provide therapeutic or eradicant action as well as protection. Botanical insecticides such as pyrethrum and rotenone have a shorter residual effect on pests, but are considered generally safer for the user and the environment than inorganic chemical insecticides.

Biological control through the use of organisms like *Bacillus thuringiensis* (a bacterium toxic to moth and butterfly larvae) is effective and safe. Recommended pesticides may vary to some extent from region to region, so consult your local Agricultural Experiment Station or plant professional about the appropriate material to use. Always read the pesticide label to be sure that it is registered for use on roses and on the pest with which you are dealing. Follow the label recommendations regarding safety precautions, dosage, and frequency of application. Learn about the life cycle of the pest, so that you know when to begin—and when to stop—spraying.

ARRANGING CUT ROSES

ARRANGERS CALL the rose the "complete flower" because it provides all stages of bloom for a complete arrangement. The rose is adaptable to every occasion: It can be formal when used for weddings, in churches, and at formal teas and showers; and it can be informal any place at home, on the porch or patio, and on the office desk. Moreover, roses are suitable for all types and styles of containers; the old rule that roses should be arranged only in silver or crystal was discarded long ago. People now realize that roses are for everyone and for any setting, and they are today the most popular flower worldwide.

Gathering Roses

Before cutting roses, select the container that will hold them, and try to decide where you will be placing it. If you are a beginner, select a low bowl or horizontal container; one that is about 10 inches in diameter and 2 inches deep will do nicely. You will want to cut your roses early in the morning or after sundown in the evening. They will keep longer if the plants are thoroughly watered one-half day before cutting; make sure to water the soil deeply around the bushes.

Take a pail of cold water with you into the garden. Using sharp rose pruners, cut the stems on a slant, selecting the proper stem length for the container you will be using. Choose strong stems, some with tight buds, some one-quarter open, and the remaining ones one-half and two-thirds open. Clean the foliage with a damp paper napkin or soft cloth (not nylon), and then dry it. Place the roses in a cool place, preferably in a refrigerator at 38° to 40° F—they will keep for days in there. If you have an old refrigerator, you are in luck—the new, self-defrosting models will remove moisture from flowers and thus cause early aging.

In these early stages of rose preparation, remove most thorns and some foliage, especially thorns and foliage below the water line. Rose foliage may be added later if the arrangement calls for it.

Beginning the Arrangement

To establish the proper proportion from the start, choose a stem that is 50 percent longer than your bowl; if your bowl is 8 inches long, your stem should be 12 inches. Using a sharp needlepoint secured with floral clay, place the first stem upright, toward the left side of the bowl. Choose a second stem, approximately three-fourths the length of the first, with the bloom one-fourth to one-third open. Put it firmly in the needlepoint, slanted to the left at an angle of about 45 degrees. The third stem should be about three-fourths the length of the second stem, with the bloom two-thirds or three-fourths open. The third stem should be at a 60-degree angle to the right and in front, with the bloom lower than the bloom on the second stem. This solid, three-stem, three-position, triangular design serves as a basic foundation for a completed arrangement. You may use other lengths of roses or other foliage or flowers to fill in and complete the plan.

Make certain that all your containers, water, and plant material are clean. You may use oasis for arrangements (well soaked before using) if you do not expect the arrangement to last more than one day. If you want to use oasis for a longer period, you must recut the stems (on a slant) and add more cold water. Be sure to use good sharp needlepoints large enough to provide adequate space for the foliage stems and flowers. If some stems are too short, try using florists' picks (small vials filled with water).

A word of caution: Never place cut roses in hot water, since they will not last. Clean cold water in clean containers is all you need to preserve the roses and all plant materials. (Flower preservatives seem to help the arranger more than the flowers themselves.) Change the water and cut the stems a little each day, otherwise, the stems may become clogged and decay. Keep cut roses out of the sun. With this care, cut roses will last a week or longer.

Design Tips

Distinction is the quality all good designers strive for. It may be the result of imagination, originality, beauty, or the use of usual materials in an unusual manner. But one factor common to all distinctive designs is good grooming—that is, attention to detail in handling and preparing roses.

Learn to master mechanical techniques, keeping in mind that, in the final analysis, simplicity is a key concept. "When in doubt, leave it out" is an old but excellent rule for new and advanced arrangers alike. Don't use too much plant material; don't feel that you must put in all the flowers and foliage that you have on hand. Many times it is wise to make the arrangement, leave it for a while, then return to look at it. You will often then see some changes to be made, and most of the time you'll remove or change some of the flowers. Looking at the design through the lens of a camera is often a good way to get a fresh idea of what your arrangement needs. Other factors to consider in your choice of arrangement style or design are the kinds and sizes of other plant materials and your containers. You will also want to think about color values (lightness or darkness) and other qualities such as shapes, silhouettes, contours, and textures.

Consider also the space the arrangement will occupy. For example, if the arrangement is for a mantel, complete the design at that height in order to visualize everything from that vantage point. If it will be placed on a table, work on the design at a table or at the same height. If it is an arrangement for a church or auditorium, sit down at the far end of a room to look at your finished design. By seeing the design from the vantage point from which others will ultimately see it, you will often find ways to improve the design or placement of your arrangement.

Color

Be sure the colors of your flowers do not clash, but blend and complement each other. Remember that some colors—such as mauve, blue, and purple—recede. Use bold, bright tones in a large area. White is lovely in a church and in some auditoriums, but it needs a suitable background to be fully enjoyed. A polychromatic scheme is often appropriate for mass arrangements, whereas a monochromatic one, or a design with variations of one hue, is suitable when particular subtlety or elegance is needed.

The Influence of Geometry

Certain visual elements create certain moods. Horizontal lines suggest peace and tranquillity; vertical lines produce a sense of energy; and diagonal lines are dynamic, restless, and forceful—use these lines with restraint. A circle or oval conveys a restful or passive mood; triangles create a sense of stability. Curved lines are gracious and flexible, but avoid drooping curves, which imply instability and weakness. Bear in mind, of course, that these geometric patterns are merely a way of classifying designs. A good design does not necessarily follow a geometric pattern.

Matching Design and Placement

If the arrangement is to be placed on a dining table, be sure to finish the arrangement on both sides, front and back. Never make a table arrangement that will block a person's view. If the arrangement is for a buffet table, it may be seen from only one side, so it is not necessary to finish the back; however, you may want to use large leaves or foliage to add depth to the arrangement, as depth is important to the completeness of any design.

Healthy Roses Make Good Arrangements

Remember that good culture pays off. No matter how exquisite your arrangement, if your roses have been neglected or improperly cared for, they will not do justice to your design. It is vital to put the same effort into cultivation—proper planting, pruning, watering, and fertilizing—that you do into arranging your roses once they are cut.

Buying Containers and Vases

If you are going to purchase containers for arrangements, consider the colors and types of roses and other plant material that you will often be using. Soft, subdued pottery in a neutral color is always a fine choice. For arrangements that will look well in a gray container, use something made of lead, pewter, or silver. For yellow flowers, try gold, bronze, or brass. To bring out the orange, go with copper. Baskets are good, too, and interestingly shaped bottles lend themselves to exciting arrangements. Wooden and woven trays also suit many types of arrangements. Vases and containers with unexpected potential may be found at flea markets, Goodwill shops, thrift shops, and garage sales. Once you start arranging, you will find unusual containers for all types of designs.

Flowers and Foliages for Arrangements

Many flowers and foliages go very well with roses. Try the following: daisies, gerberas, snapdragons, love-in-a-mist (*Ni-*

gella), larkspur, delphinium (all colors), lilies (be sure they are in proportion with the size of roses you are using), gladiolus, lupine, tritoma, and veronica. Dried allium blossoms sprayed with gold or silver are like tiny stars on the stem and make beautiful arrangements with roses at Christmastime; place some holly at the base of the arrangement for a lovely holiday touch. You will find many other interesting flowers for arranging with roses.

Line Materials in Arrangements

In arranging roses, it is important to use materials that serve to extend or enhance the line within the arrangement. Line materials include: equistum (a horse tail rush); mullein (flower or seed stem); corn stalks (green or brown); forsythia (green or brown); okra stalks (green or mature); sea oats; pampas grass plumes; wild grasses; Scotch broom; wheat; *spuria* iris foliage; dried burdock; cattails; sanseveria; yucca; and Queen Anne's lace (wild carrot). Vines can often be used when a free-flowing or loose line is needed. Some vines that can be used are: ivy (English, glacier, curly, porcelain, and grape); honeysuckle; grapevine (remove the foliage); wisteria (dried and peeled, with leaves recently removed; it will add a lovely white to an arrangement); white hemlock or circuta (dried); bittersweet; and clematis (with seed pods).

Some large leaves, including the following, are used quite frequently in mass or line arrangements: hosta, canna, calla lily, saxifrage, hydrangea (dried), and fantail willow *(Salix)*. Hydrangea blossoms may also be used; try blue hydrangea blooms with blue-red roses. Some arrangements call for branches from trees and shrubs, such as Japanese quince; holly (Chinese or American); red plum; Japanese maple; Japanese fantail willow; tamarix (gives roses an airy feeling); pussy willow; white pine; cork bark *(Euonymus alatus);* highbush cranberry *(Viburnum americana);* and nandina. Trim excess leaves from branches. With some branches, such as cork bark or fantail willow, you can remove all foliage from the branches in order to reveal interesting lines, forms, colors, and textures.

Other Ideas for Arrangements

You can create distinctive rose arrangements by using feathers (especially pheasant or grouse), interesting stones or rocks, dried fungi, and unusual pieces of weathered wood or driftwood. Once you start arranging, you will find beauty in the out-of-doors that you have never really seen or noticed before.

GLOSSARY

Anchor root
A large root serving mainly to hold a plant in place in the soil.

Anther
The terminal part of a stamen, containing the pollen sacs.

Basal cane
One of the main canes of a rose bush, originating from the bud union.

Bud eye
A dormant bud in the axil of a leaf, used for propagation in bud-grafting. Also called an eye.

Bud union
The junction, usually swollen, between the understock and the top variety grafted to it, at or near soil level.

Budded
Propagated from a bud eye.

Button center
A round center in a rose blossom, formed by unexpanded petaloids in the very double roses.

Calyx
Collectively, the sepals of a flower.

Calyx tube
A tube formed partly by the united bases of the sepals and partly by the receptacle.

Confused center
A flower center whose petals are disorganized, not forming a pattern.

Corolla
Collectively, the petals of a flower.

Crown
The region of the bud union, the point near soil level where the top variety and the understock are joined.

Cultivar
A man-made variety of a plant, maintained by vegetative propagation rather than from seed.

Cupped form
In a rose bloom, having an open center, with the stamens visible.

Dead-heading
Removal of old flowers during the growing season to encourage the development of new flowers.

Disbudded
Having the side buds removed to encourage the growth of the flower at the tip of the stem.

Double
Having 24 to 50 petals.

Eye
See Bud eye.

Feeder root
One of the numerous small roots of a plant, through which moisture and nutrients are absorbed from the soil.

Filament
The threadlike lower portion of a stamen, bearing the anther.

Floriferous
Blooming profusely.

Guard petals
The outer petals of a rose, especially when these are larger than the inner petals and enclose them.

High-centered
Having the central petals longest; the classic hybrid tea rose form.

Hip
The closed and ripened receptacle of a rose, containing the seeds, and often brightly colored.

Lateral cane
A branch of a basal cane.

Leaf axil
The angle between a petiole and the stem to which it is attached.

Leaflet
One of the leaflike parts of a compound leaf.

Main shoot
A basal cane or a strong lateral cane.

Muddled center
A flower center whose petals are disorganized, not forming a pattern. A term applied to old garden roses.

Ovary
The swollen base of a pistil, in which one or more seeds develop.

Petal
One of a series of flower parts lying within the sepals and outside the stamens and pistils; in roses, the petals are large and brightly colored. Collectively termed the corolla.

Petaloids
Small, very short petals located near the center of a flower.

Petiole
The stalk of a leaf.

Pistil
The female reproductive organ of a flower, consisting of an ovary, a style, and a stigma.

Quartered
Having petals arranged in three, four, or five radial segments.

Retentive sepals
Sepals that remain attached to the apex of the receptacle after it has ripened into a hip.

Rhachis
The central axis of a compound leaf, to which the leaflets are attached.

Rootstock
See Understock.

Rugose
Having the leaf veins deeply etched into the upper surface of the leaf.

Semidouble
Having 12 to 24 petals.

Single
Of flowers, having 5 to 12 petals. Of varieties, having only one bloom per stem.

Sport
An abrupt, naturally occurring genetic change resulting in a branch that differs in appearance from the rest of the plant, or, a plant derived by propagation from such a genetically changed branch. Also called a mutation.

Stamen
The male reproductive organ of a flower, consisting of a filament and a pollen-bearing anther.

Stem
A branch of a cane, emerging from a bud eye and bearing leaves and at least one flower.

Stigma
The terminal portion of a pistil, consisting of a sticky surface to which pollen grains adhere during pollination.

Stipule
A small, leaflike appendage at the base of the petiole of a leaf.

Style
The columnar portion of a pistil, extending between the ovary and the stigma.

Sucker
A young cane emerging below the bud union and therefore representing the variety of the understock rather than the top variety.

Top variety
The variety bud-grafted to the understock, and thus the variety that will be represented by the flowers.

Understock
The plant providing the root system to which the top variety is attached in bud-grafting. Also called a rootstock.

Very double
Having more than 50 petals.

PHOTO CREDITS

Gillian Beckett, 59, 74, 81, 82, 88, 91, 95, 101, 102

Sonja Bullaty and Angelo Lomeo © Cover, 27, 29, 47, 58, 83

Stuart C. Dobson, 41, 48, 65, 66, 69, 80, 86, 92, 98

Ken Druse, 2, 25

Derek Fell, 75

P. A. Haring, 28, 35, 36, 39, 54, 55, 60, 63, 70, 71, 72, 76, 78, 79, 84, 85, 89, 103, 104

Pamela J. Harper, 26, 30, 31, 32, 33, 34, 37, 38, 42, 44, 45, 46, 49, 50, 51, 52, 53, 56, 57, 61, 62, 64, 67, 68, 87, 94, 96, 97, 100

Ann Reilly, 73

Joy Spurr, 40, 77, 99

Doug Wechsler, 43

Peggy Wingood/Courtesy of the Bermuda Rose Society, 99

INDEX

CHANTICLEER PRESS
STEWART, TABORI & CHANG

Publisher
ANDREW STEWART

Senior Editor
ANN WHITMAN

Production
KATHY ROSENBLOOM
KARYN SLUTSKY

Design
JOSEPH RUTT